SAINTS

THE FINAL COUNTDOWN

SAINTS

THE FINAL COUNTDOWN

KEN BOLD

STELLAR BOOKS

Published in 2018 by:
Stellar Books
1 Birchdale
St Mary's Road
Bowdon
Cheshire
WA14 2PW

E: info@stellarbooks.co.uk
W: www.stellarbooks.co.uk
T: 0161 928 8273
Tw: @stellarbooksllp

ISBN: 978-1910275238

A copy of this book is available in the British Library.

Cover designed by: Stellar Books

Images on the front cover reproduced by kind permission of rhphotos.com.
From left to right:
Ian Pickavance touches down to score in the 1996 Wembley Final.
Saints celebrate winning the 2006 Grand Final.
Shane Cooper holds the Premiership Trophy aloft after Saints' victory over Wigan in the 1993 final.
Tommy Makinson scores against Wigan in the 2014 Grand Final.

All profits from the sale of this book will go to the Steve Prescott Foundation.

CONTENTS

ABOUT THE AUTHOR

Ken Bold was born at Cowley Hill Hospital in St Helens in December 1952. His father was a keen Saints supporter and for many years he operated one of the turnstiles at Knowsley Road on match days. From a very early age Ken accompanied his dad to reserve games and attended his initial first team match in February 1960. He has watched many hundreds of Saints games since then and, hopefully, will continue to watch Saints for many years yet.

He played amateur Rugby League for Saints 'Youth Section' before representing Leeds University at the sport in the early seventies. He played for a number of local clubs after completing his studies, most notably Saints B team. After he finished playing he spent several years as a referee. He also coached school teams at Sutton Manor and Penketh primary schools.

He now lives in Widnes but regularly makes the short trip to the Totally Wicked Stadium to watch Saints and makes contributions to the 'Saints and Proud' matchday programme.

This is his first book.

INTRODUCTION

My first experience of attending a cup final is one of my clearest childhood memories. I was eight years old and remember walking to St Helens Shaw Street station (now St Helens Central) to catch the special excursion train to Wembley. The date was 13 May 1961. On arrival in London we took in some of the sights before travelling to Wembley. It was a hot day with glorious sunshine and the approaches to the stadium were filled with families from Wigan and St Helens wearing various forms of red and white clothing, including hats, scarves and rosettes, many of which were home-made.

The match itself is something of a blur but I distinctly remember a boy of around my age, presumably from Wigan, crying his eyes out as the final whistle approached as he realised that Saints were going to win. In contrast I felt a feeling of utter jubilation when Vince Karalius held up the gleaming trophy and the many thousands of Saints supporters cheered and shouted their congratulations.

A final is all about winners and losers. There is no opportunity for the losers to put things right, no chance of the winners having the prize removed from their grasp. Finals are binary; joy or despair, glory or gloom. Finals are sport at its most extreme, both for players and for supporters.

Over the years Saints have provided their supporters with triumph and disaster in roughly equal measures. I remember with great fondness Saints' 'Dad's Army' beating a great Widnes side at Wembley in 1976 and Bobbie Goulding's aerial bombardment of Bradford's Nathan Graham as Saints overturned a large deficit in just six unbelievable minutes at Wembley in 1996. The celebrations when 'one armed bandit' Billy Benyon collected a horribly skewed John Walsh drop goal attempt to steal the 1971 Championship from Wigan in the final seconds were ecstatic. Few who were around at the time will forget how Mal Meninga galvanised Saints in the 1984/85 season and his leading role in their Lancashire Cup final and Premiership Trophy victories. And what about Tommy Makinson's game breaking try in the 2014 Grand Final! All are memories to savour.

However there have been many disappointments too. I'm not sure which was worse, being crushed 0-27 by Wigan at Wembley in 1989 or losing 18-19 to a very ordinary Halifax side two years earlier, when Mark Elia infamously had the ball knocked from his grasp as he looked certain to score. I remember watching Saints draw against Wakefield Trinity in atrocious conditions in the 1967 Championship final and then being outplayed in the replay. The recurring nightmare of five successive defeats in the Super League Grand Final between 2007 and 2011 stands out as an extreme case of serial disappointment.

Since 1998 each Rugby League season has contained just two major finals. The Challenge Cup is the world's oldest Rugby League knock out competition and the final, especially when played at Wembley, retains a special place in the hearts and minds of every player and supporter. The Super League Grand Final, which is always played at Old Trafford in early October, is a magnificent occasion which provides the climax to every domestic season.

However, there have been many other competitions in the history of the game which have required finals to determine the winners. Between 1906/07 and 1961/62 the Championship winners were determined by the winners of a play-off between the top four clubs which culminated in a final. After a short lived two division experiment the top 16 clubs took part in a knock-out play-off leading to a Championship final in the seasons from 1964/65 until 1972/73. From 1974/75 until 1996/97 the knock-out Premiership Trophy was competed for by the season's leading teams. Imperial Tobacco sponsored a knock out competition run on similar lines to the Challenge Cup, but without the same prestige and history, which ran from 1971/72 until 1995/96. The Lancashire and Yorkshire cups were highlights of the first half of each season between 1905/06 and 1992/93. Saints featured in nineteen Lancashire Cup finals, including the very last one, played in front of a full house at Knowsley Road. Older supporters will have fond memories of the BBC2 Floodlit Trophy which was played between October and December of each year between 1965 and 1979. Saints also appeared in the only Club Championship final, held at the end of the 1973/74 season, and won the Western Region final in 1963/64.

The World Club Challenge does not feature in this book as the matches were not finals but simply one-off matches between the champion sides of Great Britain and Australia. For similar reasons the short-lived European Championship is not included either.

I hope that readers will enjoy reading the accounts of every one of the 79 finals, and two replays, in which Saints have played. For some they will jog memories of matches they attended, for others they will provide what I intend to be an interesting insight into the long and proud history of St Helens Rugby League Club. Let's hope there are many more final appearances in the years to come!

CHALLENGE CUP FINALS

This knock out competition was first contested in 1897 and apart from war time breaks has been held in every season since then.

- Saints have played in 21 finals, winning twelve and losing nine
- Saints' highest score is 42 v Huddersfield Giants (2006)
- Opponents' highest score is 37 v Huddersfield (1915)
- Saints' biggest margin of victory is 30 v Huddersfield Giants (2006)
- Saints' biggest margin of defeat is 34 v Huddersfield (1915)
- The highest attendance at any Challenge Cup Final in which Saints have played is 98,536 v Wigan (1966), which is the highest ever attendance at any match in which Saints have played.
- The lowest attendance at any Challenge Cup Final in which Saints have played is 8,000 v Huddersfield (1915)
- 15 of the finals have been played at Wembley. The other venues have been Headingley, Leeds (1897), Fartown, Huddersfield (1915), Twickenham, London (2001 and 2006), Millennium, Cardiff (2004) and Murrayfield, Edinburgh (2002)
- Saints won on all five visits to Wembley between 1956 and 1976. They only conceded one try in this period, Phil Cookson scoring for Leeds in 1972
- 59 years passed between Saints' first Challenge Cup Final appearance (1897) and their first final victory (1956)

1897 CHALLENGE CUP FINAL

SATURDAY 24 APRIL at HEADINGLEY, LEEDS

SAINTS v BATLEY

SAINTS	BATLEY
Tommy FOULKES (Capt)	Arthur GARNER
Bob DOHERTY	Wharton DAVIES
David TRAYNOR *Try*	Dai FITZGERALD
Jim BARNES	Jack GOODALL (Capt) *Try*
Billy JACQUES	Ike SHAW
Robert O'HARE	Joe OAKLAND *DG*
Fred LITTLE	Harry GOODALL
Tom WINSTANLEY	Mark SHACKLETON
William 'Kitty' BRIERS	Jim GATH
William WINSTANLEY	George MAINE
Tom REYNOLDS	Bob SPURR
Joe THOMPSON	Fred FISHER
Peter DALE	Charlie STUBLEY
Sam RIMMER	Jack LITTLEWOOD
Bill WHITELEY	John MUNNS *Try*

Referee: Mr J. H. Smith (Widnes) Attendance: 13,492

1896/97 was the second season of the recently formed Northern Union and it had been decided to organise a knock out competition at the conclusion of the league season, with the semi-finals and final to be held at neutral venues.

Saints were fortunate to be given home ties in each of the first four rounds. They thrashed junior side Lees 58-0 in the first round and then comfortably defeated Castleford 17-3 in the second. Local rivals Wigan were dispatched 11-0 in the third round and then Tyldesley were beaten 12-0 in the fourth to earn Saints a semi-final against Swinton, which was held at Broughton. Saints triumphed by 7 points to nil in front of over 20,000 spectators to earn a place in the inaugural Northern Union Challenge Cup Final.

Saints' progress to the final had been impressive, scoring 105 points and only conceding three. However, opponents Batley were favourites to win, possibly because their proximity to Leeds enabled more of their supporters to attend the game. Surprisingly, neither side had had impressive league seasons. Saints had only finished ninth in the Lancashire Senior Competition and Batley sixth in the Yorkshire section, but both had deservedly fought their way through to the final.

Whilst Batley wore smart white jerseys, Saints wore the same faded blue and white striped jerseys that they had worn throughout the competition. Their respective kits mirrored the teams' performances on the day. Batley played the smarter, more organised rugby throughout, whilst Saints' play was much less sharp. The game was fifteen-a-side and the rules were very similar to those in operation in rugby union.

Three trainloads of Saints supporters only arrived at the ground midway through the first half due to delays. By then Saints were already 0-7 down!

Batley opened the scoring in the fourth minute when Oakland landed a drop goal, which was worth four points. Jack Goodall scored the game's first try in the fifteenth minute when he collected a cross-field kick but the conversion was missed. Fred Little came close to scoring a try but was hauled down close to the Batley line and Billy Jacques narrowly missed a penalty attempt. Batley too had opportunities but there were no further scores in the first half.

Saints scored the game's best try in the 55th minute. Bob Doherty fielded a Batley kick and made good ground before passing to David Traynor who showed great pace and power to complete a fifty yard run to the line. Although the conversion was missed Saints were back in the game at 3-7 down. However, Batley continued to dominate and it was no surprise when Munns scored their second try in the corner with fifteen minutes to go.

Most observers agreed that the better team had won but Saints had still managed to take their place in history by playing in the first ever Challenge Cup final. However, few in the crowd would live to see the day when they actually managed to win the trophy.

SAINTS 3 - BATLEY 10

Match ball (© Copyright Alex Service)

Northern Rugby Football Union.

CHALLENGE CUP—FINAL TIE.

BATLEY V. ST. HELENS

At Headingley, Leeds, on Saturday, April 24th, 1897.

KICK OFF 3-30 PROMPT.

ADMIT TO GROUND AND ENCLOSURE.

J. PLATT, HON. SEC.

Match ticket (© Copyright Curtis Johnstone)

FINAL FACT

As this was the first ever Challenge Cup final a new trophy was required. It was supplied by Fattorini and Sons and cost £60.

1915 CHALLENGE CUP FINAL

SATURDAY 1 MAY at WATERSHEDDINGS, OLDHAM

SAINTS v HUDDERSFIELD

SAINTS	HUDDERSFIELD
Bert ROBERTS	Major HOLLAND *Try*
Tommy BARTON (Capt)	Albert ROSENFIELD *Try*
Jimmy FLANAGAN	Tommy GLEESON *Try*
Tom WHITE	Harold WAGSTAFFE (Capt) *2 Tries*
Henry GREENALL	Stanley MOORHOUSE *2 Tries*
Matt CREEVEY	Bert GANLEY *Try*
Fred TREMWITH	Johnny ROGERS
George FARRIMOND	Willy HIGSON
Sam DANIELS *Try*	Aaron LEE
James SHALLCROSS	Fred LONGSTAFF
William JACKSON	Herbert BANKS
Tom DURKIN	Ben GRONOW *Try and 5 Goals*
Billy MYERS	Douglas CLARK

Referee: Mr R. Robinson (Bradford) Attendance: 8,000

The 1915 Challenge Cup final was a mismatch between a Saints side depleted by many players volunteering to serve in the armed forces and demoralised by the financially stricken state of the club and Huddersfield's 'Team of all the talents' which was the finest team assembled since the birth of the game. Huddersfield had topped the league table for the fourth successive season, losing only two of the thirty-four league games that they played. They had hammered Leeds 35-2 in the Championship final and had also won the Yorkshire League and Yorkshire Cup.

There had been much debate as to whether the 1914/15 season should go ahead at all in view of the outbreak of the Great War. After much discussion and soul searching it was decided that the season should continue as planned but that clubs should encourage players and supporters to enlist to serve king and country. In the first four months of the war fourteen Saints players did so, compared with just two from Huddersfield. Crowds and enthusiasm for the game fell sharply and the club's finances were in a very parlous state.

Saints played five games en route to the final and never scored more than nine points in any of them. They were, at best, a workmanlike side with a resolute defence. They overcame junior side Featherstone 6-0 in the first round and then edged past Swinton 5-0 in the second. They were drawn away for the third time in succession and travelled to Keighley in the quarter final, scraping a 3-2 victory over the Yorkshire side. The semi-final against Rochdale Hornets was drawn 5-5 but to the surprise of many Saints won the replay 9-2 to reach the Challenge Cup final for the second time in the club's history.

Only 8,000 spectators attended the final at Watersheddings in Oldham. Saints' players were told shortly before kick-off that there would no bonuses paid even in the unlikely event of a victory and many were on the point of refusing to play. Fortunately, captain Tommy Barton's rousing speech in the dressing room convinced them all to play but inevitably morale was low for what should have been the highlight of their careers.

The game was only two and a half minutes old when Gleeson scored Huddersfield's first try. Saints defended stoutly for twenty minutes until Wagstaffe scored the second try and Gronow converted to put Huddersfield 8-0 up. The game was as good as over by half time as Huddersfield scored three further tries and two goals to open up a 21-0 lead. Huddersfield continued to dominate the second half and scored four further tries and two more goals to record 37 points. This remained a record Challenge Cup final score until 1960. Sam Daniels scored Saints' only try late in the game.

SAINTS 3 - HUDDERSFIELD 37

Huddersfield's star player, Harold Wagstaffe, gave his shirt to Saints captain Tom Barton after the match.
(© Copyright Alex Service)

FINAL FACT

Jimmy Flanagan (Saints) and Fred Longstaffe (Huddersfield) were amongst many of the players who joined the armed forces.
Very sadly, both were killed in action.

1930 CHALLENGE CUP FINAL

SATURDAY 3 MAY at WEMBLEY

SAINTS v WIDNES

SAINTS	WIDNES
Charlie CROOKS	Bob FRASER
Alf ELLABY	Jack DENNETT *Try*
Bill MERCER	Albert RATCLIFFE *Try and Goal*
George LEWIS	Peter TOPPING
Roy HARDGRAVE	Harry OWEN
Les FAIRCLOUGH	Paddy DOUGLAS
Walter GROVES	Jerry LAUGHTON
Lou HUTT	Fred KELSALL
Bill CLAREY	George STEVENS
Lou HOUGHTON *Try*	Nat SILCOCK
Trevor HALL	George VAN ROOYEN
Ben HALFPENNY	Harry MILLINGTON
Bob HARRISON	Jimmy HOEY *Goal*

Referee: Mr F Peel | Attendance: 36,544

The Saints side of the 1929/30 season was the strongest yet assembled by the club. Saints had topped the league table for the first time ever but lost at home to Leeds in the Championship play-off semi-final the week before the Challenge Cup final. They travelled to London as strong favourites to defeat Widnes, whose team consisted of twelve local lads and a veteran South African, Van Rooyen. The Chemics had finished in the lower half of the table and had surprised many by reaching the final for the first time in their club's history.

Saints' Challenge Cup run started with a derby against local rivals St Helens Recs at Knowsley Road. As was often the case, there was little to choose between the teams but in a tight game Saints managed a 9-7 victory to earn a trip to Leeds in the second round, where they triumphed by 18 points to 5. Saints' reward was a home tie against Hunslet, which they won 22-7. Their semi-final opponents were Wigan. The two rivals fought out a 5-5 draw at Swinton in front of 37,169 spectators- more than attended the final! 24,000 crammed into Leigh's ground to watch Saints win the replay 22-10 and qualify for their first trip to Wembley.

Saints started strongly and when the Widnes defence failed to deal effectively with a kick through by Alf Ellaby, prop forward Lou Houghton dived on the loose ball to open the scoring. However, Widnes soon took the lead with a converted try. Charlie Crookes dropped Ratcliffe's kick and then compounded his error by obstructing him as he chased the ball. The referee had no hesitation in awarding a penalty try and Widnes were 5-3 in front following the conversion. Saints were struggling to find any rhythm or cohesion in their play and Dennet extended Widnes' lead with a try in the 33rd minute. A Hoey penalty completed the first half scoring and so Widnes led 10-3 at the break.

It was a warm, sunny day and Saints appeared to be lethargic in the second half and their play lacked urgency and fluency. Star winger Ellaby blamed this on being 'jiggered' from too much sightseeing around the capital prior to the game. Whatever the cause, the Widnes line was never seriously threatened, although Saints did carve out a few openings. However, the Chemics held on with comparative ease to complete an unexpected victory that is still regarded as one of the finest in Widnes' history.

The teams travelled back up north on the same train but it was Widnes who shared their carriage with the famous trophy. Saints reached the semi-finals in 1931 and 1933 but lost on each occasion. Their supporters would have to wait until 1953 for the club's second appearance at the Empire Stadium.

SAINTS 3 - WIDNES 10

FINAL FACT

The attendance of 36,544 remains the lowest of any Challenge Cup final played at Wembley. It was almost 5,000 less than the previous year's inaugural Wembley final crowd.

1953 CHALLENGE CUP FINAL

SATURDAY 25 APRIL at WEMBLEY

SAINTS v HUDDERSFIELD

SAINTS	**HUDDERSFIELD**
Glyn MOSES	John HUNTER
Steve LLEWELLYN *Try*	Peter HENDERSON
Duggie GREENALL (Capt)	Russell PEPPERELL (Capt)
Don GULLICK	Pat DEVERY *Goal*
Stan McCORMICK	Lionel COOPER 2 *Goals*
Jimmy HONEY	Peter RAMSDEN 2 *Tries*
George LANGFIELD *Try, Goal, DG*	Billy BANKS *Try*
Alan PRESCOTT	Ted SLEVIN
Reg BLAKEMORE	George CURRAN
George PARR	Jim BOWDEN
George PARSONS	Jack BROWN
Bill BRETHERTON	Jack LARGE
Ray CALE	Dave VALENTINE
Coach: Jim Sullivan	Player Coach: Russell Pepperell

Referee: Mr G. Phillips (Widnes) Attendance: 89,588

Saints supporters went to Wembley in 1953 with high hopes that the team would bring the famous Challenge Cup trophy home for the first time ever. Saints had lured Jim Sullivan from Wigan to become the club's coach and had spent extensively to put together what was felt to be the club's finest side since the inception of the game. Saints had finished top of the league table, dropping only six points in thirty-six games. However, three of these points had been to their cup final opponents, Huddersfield.

Interest in Rugby League in general and the Challenge Cup in particular were at an all-time high. A total of 51,000 spectators attended the two legs of Saints' first round tie with Oldham. Saints won 20-4 at home and then drew 5-5 at Watersheddings to secure a second round tie at home to struggling Belle Vue Rangers, whom they defeated 28-0 in front of a crowd of 20,000. 32.051 crammed into Leigh's ground to watch Saints win their quarter-final 12-3. Station Road, Swinton was the venue for the semi-final against Warrington. Over 38,000 witnessed a tight game which Saints won 9-3. The crowds for Huddersfield's games were even bigger. Over 69,000 watched their quarter final at Bradford and more than 58,000 attended their semi-final victory over Wigan at the same stadium.

The final was a very physical encounter which bordered on the brutal at times. In the view of most neutral observers Huddersfield were more sinned against than sinners and Hunter and Ramsden both had to leave the field for treatment to injuries. However, both returned and played significant roles in Huddersfield's victory.

The first half hour was dominated by robust tackling from both sides. Devery missed three penalty kicks for Huddersfield and Langfield missed one for Saints. Ramsden opened the scoring when he bounced over for a try after appearing to be tackled just short of the line. Saints fans were convinced that there had been a double movement but referee George Phillips did not share their view. Devery's conversion put the Yorkshire side 5-0 up. In the 38th minute George Langfield kicked a penalty and from the resulting kick off Glyn Moses, Stan McCormick and Duggie Greenall combined well to break through the Huddersfield defence and Steve Llewellyn finished the move in style in the corner. However, Langfield missed the conversion and the sides went in level at 5-5 at half time.

Langfield broke the deadlock on the hour mark with a good try but unfortunately couldn't land the conversion. Soon afterwards Hunter was stretchered off following a tackle which angered Huddersfield supporters. However, Banks scooted down the blind side from a scrum to score and Cooper's conversion put Huddersfield ahead. Langfield then landed a drop goal to square things up at 10 all. The tension was almost unbearable as both sides tried to deliver the knockout blow. With just four minutes remaining Valentine and Bowden created space for Ramsden, who scored his second try on what was his nineteenth birthday. Cooper's conversion put the Yorkshire side 15-10 ahead and they almost added to their lead in the last minute but the referee disallowed Cooper's 'try' for a forward pass before blowing his whistle for full time.

56 years had passed since Saints had lost the inaugural Challenge Cup final and still their supporters had not been able to celebrate a victory.

SAINTS 10 - HUDDERSFIELD 15

Man of the match: Peter Ramsden

FINAL FACT

George Langfield's successful 38th minute penalty kick was Saints' first ever Challenge Cup final goal. In each one of their three previous appearances they had only scored unconverted tries.

The 1953 Challenge Cup final programme cover appears to show a Saints player diving in for a try.

George Parsons, Duggie Greenall, John 'Todder' Dickinson, Reg Blakemore and George Parr pose with a photograph of Saints' 1953 Challenge Cup final squad in 2003.
(© Copyright Alex Service)

Saints players and officials proudly pose with the Challenge Cup after winning it for the first time ever in 1956
(© Copyright Saints Heritage Society).

1956 CHALLENGE CUP FINAL

SATURDAY 28 APRIL at WEMBLEY

SAINTS v HALIFAX

SAINTS	HALIFAX
Glyn MOSES	Tyssul GRIFFITHS *Goal*
Steve LLEWELLYN *Try*	Arthur DANIELS
Duggie GREENALL	Tommy LYNCH
Brian HOWARD	Geoff PALMER
Frank CARLTON *Try*	Johnny FREEMAN
Bill FINNAN	Ken DEAN
Austin RHODES 2 *Goals*	Stan KIELTY
Alan PRESCOTT (Capt) *Try*	Jack WILKINSON
Len McINTYRE	Alvin ACKERLEY (Capt)
Nat SILCOCK	John HENDERSON
George PARSONS	Albert FEARNLEY
Roy ROBINSON	Les PEARCE
Vince KARALIUS	Ken TRAILL
Coach: Jim Sullivan	Coach: Frank Dawson

Referee: Mr R. Gelder (Wakefield) Attendance: 89,588

Saints supporters were cautiously optimistic that their team could finally overcome its Challenge Cup hoodoo in 1956 and lift the trophy for the first time. However, Halifax had defeated Saints 23-8 in the championship semi-final the previous weekend and star half back John 'Todder' Dickinson had sustained an injury which kept him out of the cup final.

Saints had been fortunate enough to receive home ties in the first three rounds of the competition. Warrington were beaten 15-6 in front of 23,000 supporters before Castleford were overrun 48-5 in the second round. 26,000 packed into Knowsley road for the quarter final against Bradford Northern and Saints responded with a superb 53-6 victory, Frank Carlton scoring four tries. Almost 39,000 fans squeezed into Swinton's ground to watch Saints and Barrow play out a 5-5 draw in the semi-final. 44,731 watched the replay at Wigan where Saints finally overcame their tenacious opponents by 10 points to 5.

Only five of the side that lost to Huddersfield in the 1953 final played against Halifax: Glyn Moses, Steve Llewellyn, Duggie Greenall, Alan Prescott and George Parsons.

A rule change had been introduced at the start of the season which required players to retreat three yards at the play the ball, rather than just one. Bill Fallowfield, the secretary of the league, commented in his article in the programme that 'Making players stand back makes it easier to open up play, *providing the players wish to play the open game.'* He would have been greatly disappointed by the first half, in which no points were scored and both sides appeared to be very reluctant to take any risks. Attempts to break the deadlock with penalty kicks also proved fruitless, with Austin Rhodes and Griffiths unable to find the target.

The second half continued in much the same vein until skipper Alan Prescott broke through and covered half the length of the field before losing the ball as he was tackled. Saints at last chanced their arm and fine passing created enough space for Frank Carlton to streak clear and open the scoring in the 66th minute. Rhodes managed to convert to put Saints 5-0 ahead. They appeared to gain confidence from this success and soon afterwards produced an excellent flowing move that resulted in Steve Llewellyn scoring in the right hand corner. Rhodes landed an excellent conversion to open up a ten point lead. Griffiths landed a penalty goal for Halifax but victory was sealed when Vince Karalius, playing with a badly torn ear, slipped the ball out of the tackle to Alan Prescott who reached out to score near the posts. Rhodes fluffed the easy conversion but the match was won and Prescott became the first Saints captain to receive the Challenge Cup trophy. For good measure he won the Lance Todd trophy as man of the match.

Saints supporters finally got the chance to enjoy a cup final victory after fifty-nine long years of disappointment.

SAINTS 13 - HALIFAX 2

Man of the match: Alan Prescott

FINAL FACT

Five of Saints' backs were born in St Helens, the exceptions being Welshmen Glyn Moses and Steve Llewellyn.

1961 CHALLENGE CUP FINAL

SATURDAY 13 MAY at WEMBLEY

SAINTS v WIGAN

SAINTS	**WIGAN**
Austin RHODES 3 *Goals*	Fred GRIFFITHS 3 *Goals*
Tom VAN VOLLENHOVEN *Try*	Billy BOSTON
Ken LARGE	Eric ASHTON
Brian McGINN	Geoff BOOTLE
Mick SULLIVAN	Frank CARLTON
Alex MURPHY *Try*	David BOLTON
Wilf SMITH	Terry ENTWISTLE
Abe TERRY	John BARTON
Bob DAGNALL	Bill SAYER
Cliff WATSON	Brian McTIGUE
Don VINES	Frank COLLIER
Dick HUDDART	Geoff LYON
Vince KARALIUS	Roy EVANS
Coach: Alan Prescott	Coach: Joe Egan

Referee: Mr T.W. Watkinson (Swinton) Attendance: 94,672

It had been five years since Saints' historic first-ever Challenge Cup win and in the eyes of their supporters a return trip to Wembley was overdue. However, Saints almost went out of the tournament in the first round. They were expected to beat Widnes comfortably at Knowsley Road, but the Chemics proved very dogged opponents and played out a 5-5 draw. However, Saints performed much better in the replay at Naughton Park and ran out comfortable 29-10 winners in front of over 24,000 spectators on a cool Thursday afternoon in February. A trip to Castleford was Saints' reward and they managed an 18-10 victory before defeating Swinton 17-9 at Knowsley Road in the quarter final.

Almost 43,000 spectators gathered at the Odsal Bowl to watch the semi-final against Hull, the runners up in the two previous finals. Saints played exceptionally well, scoring six tries in a 26-9 win which secured the club's fourth visit to Wembley. Considerable extra spice was added to the occasion as for the first time deadly rivals Wigan would provide the opposition.

Interest in the match was phenomenal. The attendance was higher than that of any previous Wembley final. The day of the final was one of the hottest ever recorded at Wembley, which was expected to suit a Saints backline that included Vollenhoven, Sullivan and Murphy. However, Wigan started the match as favourites as this was their third final in four years, having won the trophy in 1958 and 1959.

The first twenty minutes were rather dour as the forwards tried to wear each other down. The only score was a Griffiths penalty for Wigan. The Saints pack, which included the very inexperienced Cliff Watson, who was playing only his eleventh game of Rugby League, gave as good as they got. However, Saints supporters roared their delight when Alex Murphy darted over for a try after taking a pass from Dick Huddart and later Rhodes added a penalty goal so Saints led 5-2 at half time. The Saints players then sipped special lemonade, water and salt drinks whilst the massed bands of the Royal Marines entertained the enormous crowd.

Early in the second half Griffiths missed a relatively easy kick at goal and then Boston thought he had scored in the corner but the touch judge ruled that Rhodes' and Watson's despairing tackle had forced the Wigan winger into touch just before he put the ball down. This proved to be the crucial turning point as although Griffiths kicked a penalty, in the 63rd minute Tom Van Vollenhoven scored one of the best tries to grace the stadium. Saints were in possession deep inside their own 25 yard line when Dick Huddart spotted a gap and made a break before slipping the ball to Vollenhoven, who then fed the ball inside to Ken Large. He covered fifty yards before passing to the supporting Vollenhoven just before Ashton's cover tackle knocked him to the ground. The South African glided around to touch down behind the posts to ensure an easy conversion for Rhodes. Rhodes and Griffiths then exchanged penalties but the final outcome was in little doubt after Vollenhoven's try.

Captain Vince Karalius declared himself 'Pleased as punch' to win the trophy, which was presented by the Earl of Derby. The thirteen Saints players each received the princely sum of £75 for their efforts.

SAINTS 12 - WIGAN 6

Man of Match Award: Dick Huddart

FINAL FACT

The receipts of over £35,000 (plus £3,000 for TV rights from the BBC) were a world record for a Rugby League match.

Saints captain Vince Karalius holds the Challenge Cup aloft after Saints' 12-6 victory over Wigan at Wembley in 1961. It was only the second time that Saints had won the famous old trophy. Dick Huddart and Bob Dagnall seem very happy to bear his 14 stone 8 pounds weight despite having played eighty minutes of rugby in the searing heat.

Vince was known in Australia as the 'Wild Bull of the Pampas' after his exploits on the 1958 Great Britain tour. Dick was an excellent hard running forward who relished the open spaces of Wembley. After leaving Saints he went on to play with great success in Australia. Bob was a locally born hooker who was adept at securing more than his fair share of possession from the keenly contested scrums of the period.

Bill Sayer and Len Killeen lead the lap of honour around Wembley after the 21-2 victory over Wigan in the 1966 Challenge Cup final. On the right is John Mantle.

Bill had been signed earlier in the season from Wigan and proved to be an excellent acquisition. He helped Saints to dominate possession from the scrums and this proved to be a crucial factor in Saints' win. He had played for Wigan against Saints in the 1961 final.

Len Killeen was a worthy winner of the Lance Todd trophy, having scored a try and kicked five goals. He also scored all of Saints' twelve points in their semi-final victory against Dewsbury.

John Mantle was one of many excellent Welsh players who played for Saints in the sixties and seventies. He scored one of Saints' three tries in the final.

1966 CHALLENGE CUP FINAL

SATURDAY 21 MAY at WEMBLEY

SAINTS v WIGAN

SAINTS	WIGAN
Frank BARROW	Ray ASHBY
Tom VAN VOLLENHOVEN	Billy BOSTON
Alex MURPHY *DG*	David STEPHENS
Billy BENYON	Eric ASHTON
Len KILLEEN *Try and 5 goals*	Trevor LAKE
Peter HARVEY	Cliff HILL
Tommy BISHOP *Try*	Frank PARR
Albert HALSALL	Danny GARDINER
Bill SAYER	Tom WOOSNEY
Cliff WATSON	Brian McTIGUE
Ray FRENCH	Anthony STEPHENS
John WARLOW	Laurie GILFEDDER *Goal*
John MANTLE *Try*	Harry MAJOR
Substitutes	Substitutes
Tony BARROW	Chris HESKETH
Jeff HITCHEN	Geoff LYON
Coach: Joe Coan	Player Coach: Eric Ashton

Referee: H.G. Hunt (Warrington) Attendance: 98,536

Five years had passed since Saints had defeated Wigan in the 1961 final. In the intervening years Wigan had twice visited Wembley, losing to Wakefield Trinity and defeating Hunslet.

The first round draw had given Saints a difficult away tie at Wakefield Trinity but they won a tight game 10-0 in front of over 20,000 spectators. An even larger crowd watched their second round match at Knowsley Road when visitors Swinton were defeated by 16 points to 4. However, Saints looked to be heading out of the competition when they trailed Hull KR 7-10 at Knowsley Road in the third round with only seconds left. A high Alex Murphy kick bounced awkwardly over the Rovers line and he pounced on the loose ball to score, with Len Killeen's conversion securing a fortunate but very welcome victory.

Saints faced unfancied Dewsbury in the semi-final at Swinton and were expected to win easily. The game was a rough one as Dewsbury played a very physical game to counteract Saints' more skilful approach. Len Killeen scored all of Saints' points in a 12-5 victory.

Saints had three of the 1961 winning team in their line up for the final: Tom Van Vollenhoven, Alex Murphy and Cliff Watson. Crucially, they had signed one of Wigan's 1961 team, hooker Bill Sayer, earlier in the season. Boston, Ashton and McTigue had also played in the 1961 final. Wigan started the game without a specialist hooker as Colin Clarke had been sent off in a previous game and was suspended for the final, so utility forward Tom Woosney was drafted in as a makeshift hooker. The stadium was full to capacity and the crowd remains the largest ever for a Rugby League Cup Final at Wembley.

Saints led 9-2 at half time, thanks to a John Mantle try and three Len Killeen goals, including one monster kick from inside his own half. Gilfedder scored Wigan's only points with a penalty. A key feature of Saints' tactics had been to deliberately go offside when Wigan were in possession in their own half. The only option open to Wigan was to punt the ball into touch and more often than not Saints would heel the ball from the resulting scrum, thus gaining possession. There was no limit on the number of tackles the side in possession could keep the ball and consequently Saints dominated possession whilst Wigan spent much of the half tackling.

This pattern continued in the second half. In the 54th minute a cute grubber kick from Billy Benyon was touched down by Killeen and a quarter of an hour later Tommy Bishop sealed victory with a try under the posts. Len Killeen kicked a total of five goals and was awarded the Lance Todd trophy. In the final minute Alex Murphy added a trademark drop goal to complete a comprehensive victory.

Whilst Saints supporters were delighted with the day's events many neutrals were not. The following season the penalty rule was changed so that play was restarted with a tap penalty rather than a scrum after a penalty kick to touch. In addition the unlimited tackle rule was abolished and the four tackle rule introduced, which would have a dramatic effect on the way the game was played in the future.

SAINTS 21 - WIGAN 2

Man of Match Award: Len Killeen

FINAL FACT

The attendance of 98,536 exceeded that at the FIFA World Cup Final between England and West Germany held later that summer by 1,612.

1972 CHALLENGE CUP FINAL

SATURDAY 13 MAY at WEMBLEY

SAINTS v LEEDS

SAINTS	LEEDS
Geoff PIMBLETT	John HOLMES
Les JONES *Try*	Alan SMITH
Billy BENYON	Sid HYNES
Johnny WALSH	Les DYL
Frank WILSON	John ATKINSON
Ken KELLY	Alan HARDISTY (Capt)
Jeff HEATON	Keith HEPWORTH
Graham REES *Try*	Terry CLAWSON *5 Goals*
Les GREENALL	Tony FISHER
John STEPHENS	Bill RAMSEY
John MANTLE	Phil COOKSON *Try*
Eric CHISNALL	Bob HAIGH
Kel COSLETT (Capt) *4 Goals and DG*	Ray BATTEN
Substitutes	Substitutes
Alan WHITTLE	John LANGLEY
Kelvin EARL	Graham ECCLES
Coach: Jim Challinor	Coach: Derek Turner

Referee: E Lawrinson (Warrington) Attendance: 89,495

Saints' 1972 cup campaign could hardly have started in a lower key fashion. Saints managed an unconvincing 8-6 victory at Oldham in front of just 3,391 spectators. Their form was much better in the second round when a Frank Wilson hat trick was a key contribution in a 32-9 defeat of Huddersfield at Knowsley Road. A rare visit to York was Saints' reward and they won easily by 32 points to 5 to secure a semi-final tie with Warrington. Despite Warrington scoring the only two tries of the match, Saints managed to draw 10-10 at Central Park. The teams returned to the same venue just four days later and a bumper crowd of 32,180 saw Saints triumph 10-6.

Favourites Leeds were an outstanding side who had added the ex-Castleford 'H bombs' half back pairing of Hardisty and Hepworth to what was already a very formidable side. They were determined to atone for their shock defeat by Leigh in the previous year's final.

Tony Karalius and Eric Prescott were both injured in the previous weekend's match and the Saints pack had to be re-jigged. Les Greenall stepped in as hooker and John Stephens was added to the second row, Kelvin Earl taking his place on the substitute bench. John Mantle played with twelve stitches in his head following a car accident and wore a scrum cap. He and Billy Benyon were the only survivors of the 1966 winning team.

The four tackle rule was in force in 1972 and this had led to more kicking, both in open play and in attempts at goal, than in games played under the unlimited tackles rule.

Saints got off to the best possible start when in the very first minute veteran prop forward Graham Rees charged down an attempted clearance kick by Hepworth and touched down for a try which was converted by Kel Coslett. Winger Les Jones scored a second try in the 16th minute and Coslett kicked two further first half goals, whilst Clawson landed three for Leeds, so Saints went in at half time 12-6 to the good.

Leeds started the second half strongly and Cookson powered over for a try by the posts. However, crucially Clawson missed the easy conversion. A penalty and a drop goal (which still counted as 2 points), both from the boot of Lance Todd trophy winner Coslett, put Saints 16-9 ahead after an hour's play. Saints then defended well but Clawson, who had a somewhat erratic day with his kicking, scored two more goals to ensure a tense end to the game. Saints supporters yelled their relief when Eric Lawrinson blew the final whistle and a 16-13 victory was secured.

Kel Coslett, one of four Welshmen in the side, was delighted to receive the trophy from Mr Annenberg, the American Ambassador. He later said 'It was a big thing and a big day for me because I had missed the 1966 final through injury and in those days you didn't go to Wembley too many times in your career. It was the icing on the cake.'

SAINTS 16 - LEEDS 13

Man of the Match: Kel Coslett

FINAL FACT

Saints prop Graham Rees scored a try after just 26 seconds and this is generally accepted to be the quickest ever try in a Challenge Cup final.

1976 CHALLENGE CUP FINAL

SATURDAY 8 MAY at WEMBLEY

SAINTS v WIDNES

SAINTS	WIDNES
Geoff PIMBLETT 3 *Goals 2 DG*	Ray DUTTON 2 *Goals*
Les JONES	Alan PRESCOTT
Eddie CUNNINGHAM *Try*	Eric HUGHES
Derek NOONAN	Mick GEORGE
Roy MATHIAS	David JENKINS
Billy BENYON	David ECKERSLEY
Jeff HEATON *Try*	Reg BOWDEN
John MANTLE	Nick NELSON
Tony KARALIUS	Keith ELWELL *DG*
Kel COSLETT	John WOOD
George NICHOLLS	John FORAN
Eric CHISNALL	Mick ADAMS
Dave HULL	Doug LAUGHTON
Substitutes	Substitutes
Peter GLYNN 2 *Tries*	Denis O'NEILL
Mel JAMES	Barry SHERIDAN
Coach: Eric Ashton	Coach: Frank Myler

Referee: Mr R Moore (Wakefield) Attendance: 89,982

Saints were handed a tough first round draw away at Hull but manged to edge through with a 5-3 victory. Their reward was an even more difficult assignment; a trip to Salford. Salford were the glamour team of this era and would be crowned Champions later that year. However, Saints played very well and secured their passage to the next round with an impressive 17-11 victory. Oldham visited Knowsley Road in the quarter final and were beaten by 17 points to 9.

Saints fans were delighted when their team was drawn to play unfancied Keighley in the semi-final. A comfortable victory was judged to be a formality and as a result fewer than 10,000 spectators attended the match, which was played at Fartown, Huddersfield. However, Keighley defended as if their lives depended on it and proved to be much more difficult opponents than had been anticipated. Saints sneaked through by 5 points to 4, with scrum half Jeff Heaton scoring the game's only try.

Saints went into the final as underdogs. Widnes had won the previous year's final and the Saints squad was felt by many to be too old to compete for the full eighty minutes on a very hot spring day. Six of Saints' starting thirteen were over 30; skipper Kel Coslett and prop forward John Mantle were both 34.

However, Saints opened the scoring with an Eddie Cunningham try converted by Geoff Pimblett. Two Dutton penalties and a Pimblett drop goal completed the first half scoring and Saints led 6-4 at half time.

Elwell and Pimblett both kicked drop goals and with twelve minutes remaining the game was finely balanced at 7 points to 5. However, Jeff Heaton scampered over after taking an inside pass from Tony Karalius to score under the posts and Pimblett landed the simple conversion to give Saints some breathing space. Youngster Peter Glynn had been introduced from the substitutes' bench to replace Billy Benyon. Widnesian Glynn soon found gaps in the tiring Widnes defence. His try in the 74th minute clinched victory and he then collected his own kick to score again and became the first Saints player to score two tries in a Challenge Cup final. By the end Saints were coasting and Widnes were well beaten. When Kel Coslett received the trophy from Margaret Thatcher few of the thousands of ecstatic Saints supporters would have predicted that it would be twenty long years before Saints won another Challenge Cup final.

Between 1956 and 1976 Saints appeared in five Challenge Cup finals and won the lot. They scored fourteen tries and, incredibly, only conceded one. A whole generation of Saints fans had grown to assume that all trips to Wembley took place on sunny days and had happy endings. However, 1976 signalled the end of this golden era. Saints' next four visits to Wembley would end in defeat.

SAINTS 20 - WIDNES 5

Man of the match: Geoff Pimblett

FINAL FACT

The Lance Todd trophy was won by the winning side's full back for the third successive year. Derek Whitehead (Warrington) won in 1974 and Ray Dutton (Widnes) won in 1975.

SATURDAY, 8 MAY, 1976

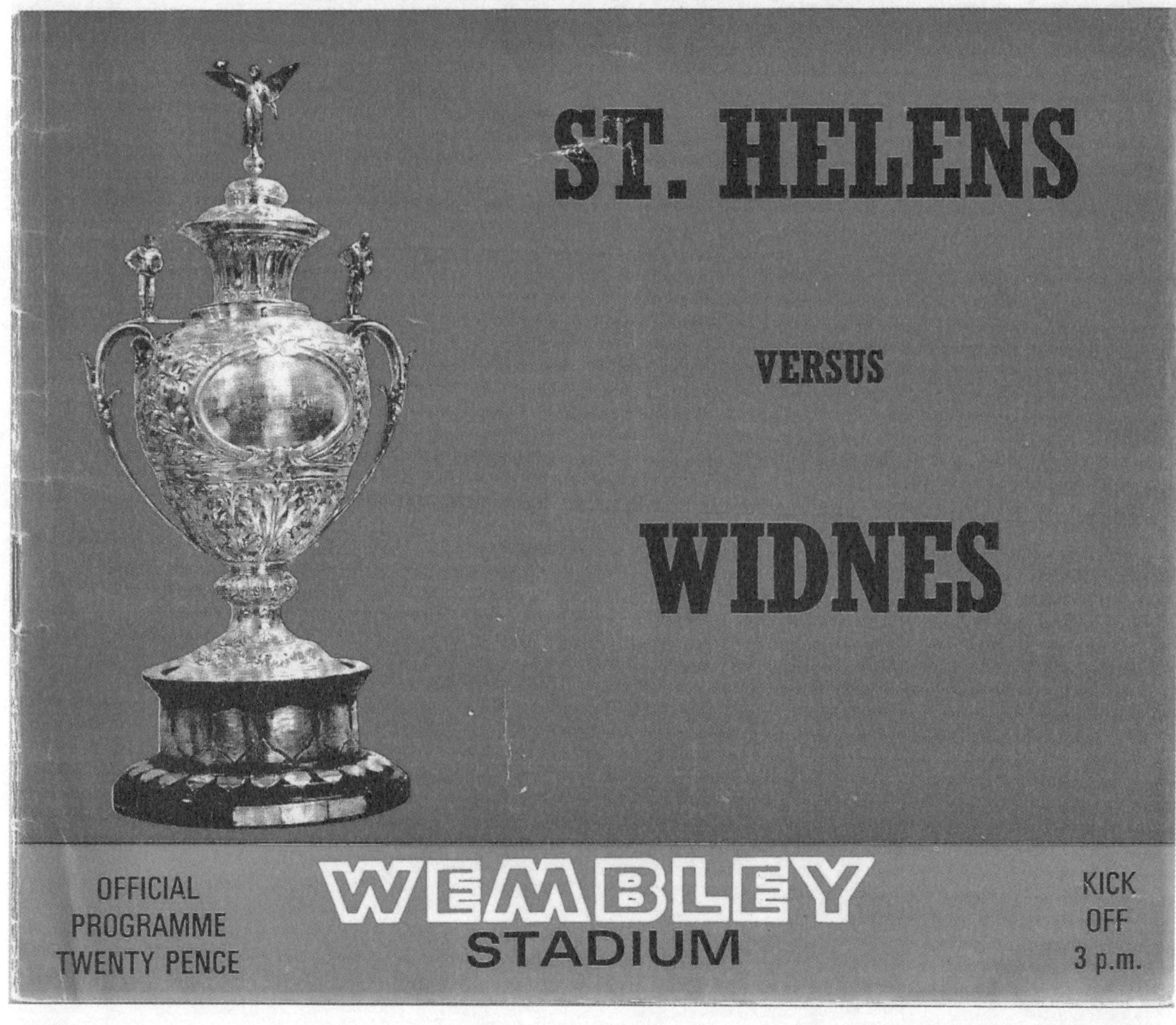

The iconic twin towers and the original trophy featured on the cover of the 1976 Challenge Cup final programme.

Photos from semi-finals between Leeds and Featherstone Rovers and Saints and Warrington were shown the cover of the 1978 Challenge Cup final programme.

1978 CHALLENGE CUP FINAL

SATURDAY 13 MAY at WEMBLEY

SAINTS v LEEDS

SAINTS	LEEDS
Geoff PIMBLETT (Capt) *3 Goals*	Willie OULTON *Goal*
Les JONES	David SMITH *Try*
Derek NOONAN	Neil HAGUE
Peter GLYNN	Les DYL
Roy MATHIAS	John ATKINSON *Try*
Bill FRANCIS *Try*	John HOLMES *DG*
Ken GWILLIAM	Sammy SANDERSON
Dave CHISNALL	Mick HARRISON
Graham LIPTROT *Try*	David WARD (Capt) *2 DG*
Mel JAMES	Steve PITCHFORD
George NICHOLLS	Graham ECCLES
Eddie CUNNINGHAM	Phil COOKSON *Try*
Harry PINNER	Mick CRANE
Substitutes	Substitutes
Alan ASHTON	Kevin DICK
Tony KARALIUS	Roy DICKINSON
Coach: Eric Ashton	Coach: Syd Hynes

Referee: Mr Thompson (Huddersfield) Attendance: 96,000

Saints comfortably defeated Huyton 36-8 at Knowsley Road to secure a place in the second round. They then travelled to Watersheddings and beat Oldham by 26 points to 11 before defeating Huddersfield 31-5 at home in the quarter final. Saints' passage to the semi -finals had been a comfortable one but defeating Warrington in order to secure another trip to Wembley was always going to be a much more difficult challenge. Over 16,000 spectators attended the semi-final at Wigan and Saints edged a tough battle 12-8 thanks to two Roy Matthias tries.

The match was dubbed the Queen's Silver Jubilee Challenge Cup final. Royalty in the form of Princess Margaret attended the event and she received a cheque for £10,000, this being the RFL's donation to the Silver Jubilee fund, and later presented the trophy to the winning captain. Although the Leeds side was not as star studded as the team beaten by Saints six years earlier it was nonetheless a very competent team. Twelve of the fifteen members of the Leeds squad had played in the previous year's final, when Leeds had defeated Widnes, whilst nine of the Saints line-up had played in the 1976 final. A close match was anticipated by the capacity crowd and so it proved.

Saints opened the scoring after four minutes when a high kick was fumbled by Leeds and the ball popped up to Graham Liptrot, who touched down for the game's first try. Bill Francis then side stepped through the defence following a scrum to score Saints' second try. Geoff Pimblett converted both tries to open up a ten point lead. Leeds needed to gain a foothold in the game and did so when fine passing created enough space for Atkinson to finish in style. Oulton landed the difficult conversion. However, Saints led 12-5 at half time as Pimblett landed a penalty following a high tackle on Dave Chisnall.

Leeds captain Ward slotted over a drop goal to reduce the gap to six points as Leeds began to dominate field position. Pressure brought its reward when first Smith and then Cookson scored tries. However, Oulton missed both conversions and the scores were tied at 12-12. Stand-off Holmes edged the Yorkshire side ahead with a drop goal and then Ward scored his second to put Leeds in front 14-12. With time running out Saints launched a final attack and engineered an overlap on the right but Derek Noonan could not take Peter Glynn's pass and the chance was lost. Soon afterwards Billy Thompson's whistle sounded and for the first time in a quarter of a century Saints had been defeated at Wembley.

SAINTS 12 - LEEDS 14

Man of the match: George Nicholls

FINAL FACT

George Nicholls is the only Saints player to have won the Lance Todd trophy as a member of the losing side.

1987 CHALLENGE CUP FINAL

SATURDAY 2 MAY at WEMBLEY

SAINTS v HALIFAX

SPONSOR: SILK CUT

SAINTS	HALIFAX
Phil VEIVERS	Graham EADIE *Try*
Barry LEDGER	Scott WILSON
Paul LOUGHLIN 3 *Goals and Try*	Colin WHITFIELD 3 *Goals*
Mark ELIA *Try*	Grant RIX
Kevin McCORMACK	Wilf GEORGE *Try*
Brett CLARK	Chris ANDERSON (Capt)
Neil HOLDING	Gary STEPHENS
Tony BURKE	Graham BEEVERS
Graham LIPTROT	Seamus McCALLION *Try*
John FIELDHOUSE	Keith NELLER
Andy PLATT	Paul DIXON
Roy HAGGERTY	Mick SCOTT
Chris ARKWRIGHT (Capt)	John PENDLEBURY *DG*
Substitutes	Substitutes
Paul ROUND *Try*	Brian JULIFF
Paul FORBER	Neil JAMES
Coach: Alex Murphy	Player Coach: Chris Anderson

Referee: Mr J. Holdsworth (Kippax)

Attendance: 91,267

Remarkably, Saints' 1987 cup run was almost over before the first round was played! The number of professional clubs had grown with teams such as Fulham, Mansfield, Sheffield and Carlisle having joined the league during the previous few years. As a result a preliminary round had to be played. Six ties were drawn and Saints were paired with Swinton at Knowsley Road. As the visitors were a second division side a home victory seemed assured but Swinton gave their hosts a severe test before going down 18-16. Saints' next three ties were much more comfortable. Dewsbury were beaten by 48 points to 12 at Crown Flatt and Oldham were defeated 24-14 at Watersheddings prior to a 41-12 victory over Whitehaven at Knowsley Road.

The semi-final at Wigan against Leigh was a much tighter affair but man of the match Phil Veivers helped Saints to prevail by 14 points to 8.

As Halifax had not appeared in a Challenge Cup final since their defeat by Saints in 1956 and had last won the trophy in 1939 they started the match as underdogs. However, they were a strong side, having been RL champions in 1986. Their two star Australian players, Eadie and Anderson, were both veterans, but still possessed the skill and experience to trouble defences and organise their team mates. Hooker Graham Liptrot was Saints' only survivor from their previous Wembley appearance in 1978. The Duke of Edinburgh attended to present the trophy.

Winger George squeezed in at the corner to register the first points of the match and Whitfield landed an excellent conversion to put Halifax 6-0 ahead. Although Paul Loughlin landed a penalty goal this was to prove Saints' only score in a disappointing first half display. Seamus McCallion burrowed over from dummy half and Whitfield converted to put Halifax 12-2 ahead at the break.

Alex Murphy doubtless had a few quiet words to his charges in the dressing room during the interval and Saints opened the second half much more strongly. Mark Elia showed superb skill and speed to round Eadie for a great try and Loughlin's conversion narrowed the gap to four points. However, man of the match Eadie soon afterwards showed real strength and determination to score by the posts and Whitfield's conversion once more stretched the lead to ten points. Loughlin then dummied through for a try but crucially could not add the conversion. Pendlebury landed a drop goal before substitute Paul Round plunged over and Loughlin added the goal to leave the match excitingly poised at 19-18.

Elia scorched through but to the astonishment of Saints fans a despairing tackle by Pendlebury dislodged the ball from his grasp. Four minutes from time Elia crossed again but was brought back for a forward pass. As the clock ticked down Saints declined several opportunities to attempt a drop goal and sank to their knees in disappointment as John Holdsworth blew the final whistle. Saints had been chasing the game since George's try and had somehow failed to catch their tiring opponents.

Disappointed coach Murphy said 'We'd have won the cup if centre Mark Elia had not copied the silly Australian habit of sliding in for a try. If he'd put the ball down in the way I'd been taught as a lad, the cup would have been ours.'

SAINTS 18 - HALIFAX 19

Man of the match: Graham Eadie

FINAL FACT

The final was Rugby League's first ever million pound game, as receipts exceeded that magic figure for the very first time. When Saints and Halifax had met at Wembley 31 years earlier the receipts were less than £30,000!

1989 CHALLENGE CUP FINAL

SATURDAY 29 APRIL at WEMBLEY

SAINTS v WIGAN

SPONSOR: SILK CUT

SAINTS	WIGAN
Gary CONNOLLY	Steve HAMPSON *Try*
Michael O'CONNOR	Tony IRO
Phil VEIVERS	Kevin IRO *2 Tries*
Paul LOUGHLIN	Dean BELL
Les QUIRK	Joe LYDON *3 Goals*
Shane COOPER	Shaun EDWARDS
Neil HOLDING	Andy GREGORY *Try and DG*
Tony BURKE	Ian LUCAS
Paul GROVES	Nicky KISS
Paul FORBER	Adrian SHELFORD
Bernard DWYER	Andy PLATT
Roy HAGGERTY	Ian POTTER
Paul VAUTIN (Capt)	Ellery HANLEY (Capt) *Try*
Substitutes	Substitutes
Darren BLOOR	Denis BETTS
Stuart EVANS	Andy GOODWAY
Coach: Alex Murphy	Coach: Graham Lowe

Referee: Mr R. Tennant (Castleford)   Attendance: 78,000

Saints made comfortable progress to the semi-finals, winning 16-5 at Swinton before defeating Barrow 28-6 and Featherstone Rovers 32-3, both at Knowsley Road. The semi-final was an altogether tighter affair. Saints faced champions elect Widnes at Wigan in front of over 17,000 spectators. The lead changed hands on numerous occasions but Les Quirk's second try, four minutes from time, edged Saints home by 16 points to 14.

Saints had completed one of their poorest league seasons for many years, losing more games than they had won. However, they managed to scrape into the Premiership play-offs by securing seventh place and the weekend before Wembley had shocked Wigan with a 4-2 victory at Central Park on a saturated pitch. Saints had played this game without their Australian stars Michael O'Connor and Paul Vautin, but elected to fly them back from Australia for the Challenge Cup final.

Wigan were warm favourites, having easily beaten Halifax in the final the previous year. Their side included four New Zealanders and several British superstars such as Hanley, Gregory, Edwards and Lydon. Saints included a young amateur, Gary Connolly, at full back. Six of the squad defeated by Halifax two years earlier played for Saints, whilst Platt played for Wigan. In an interview for the match programme Wigan coach Graham Lowe said 'Wembley is always likely to bring the very best out of the truly gifted footballer because it provides the atmosphere which uplifts them. Great players invariably rise to the biggest occasions. The Wembley arena must have created and destroyed many reputations.' The match proved the wisdom of his words.

Wembley's capacity had been reduced and 78,000 spectators filled the old stadium to witness one of the most one sided finals in its history. The game was just three minutes old when Hanley broke through and fed giant centre Kevin Iro, who brushed aside several defenders to score in the corner. Lydon missed the conversion but kicked a penalty to put his side 6-0 ahead after twenty minutes. Wigan were looking increasingly dominant and Saints heaped pressure on themselves by continually dropping the ball. Hanley scored a superb individual try after 26 minutes, weaving his way through numerous defenders on a 45 yard run to the line. Lydon's conversion completed the first half scoring and Wigan led 12-0 at half time.

If the first half was a disappointment the second half was a nightmare for Saints fans. Gregory popped over a drop goal before Iro powered over for his second try. After 65 minutes Edwards made a superb break and Gregory was on hand to score by the posts. Saints continued to offer no invention in attack or resolution in defence and Wigan scored their fifth and final try when Hampson dived over in the left hand corner. By this point many Saints supporters were already making their way out of the stadium. As one bemoaned 'We were lucky to get nil.'

SAINTS 0 - WIGAN 27

Man of the match: Ellery Hanley

FINAL FACT

Saints were the first team since 1951 to fail to score a single point in a Challenge Cup final.

1991 CHALLENGE CUP FINAL

SATURDAY 27 APRIL at WEMBLEY

SAINTS v WIGAN

SPONSOR: SILK CUT

SAINTS	WIGAN
Phil VEIVERS	Steve HAMPSON
Alan HUNTE *Try*	David MYERS *Try*
Tea ROPATI	Kevin IRO
Paul LOUGHLIN	Dean BELL
Les QUIRK	Frano BOTICA *Try and 2 goals*
Jonathan GRIFFITHS	Shaun EDWARDS
Paul BISHOP 2 *Goals*	Andy GREGORY *DG*
Jonathan NEILL	Ian LUCAS
Bernard DWYER	Martin DERMOTT
Kevin WARD	Andy PLATT
John HARRISON	Denis BETTS
George MANN	Phil CLARKE
Shane COOPER (Capt)	Ellery HANLEY
Substitutes	Substitutes
Gary CONNOLLY	Bobbie GOULDING
Paul GROVES	Andy GOODWAY
Coach: Mike McClennan	Coach: John Monie

Referee: Mr J. Smith (Halifax)

Attendance: 75,532

Saints' first round tie with Swinton took place at Manchester City's Maine Road ground as Station Road was frozen. Saints were behind at half time but eventually prevailed by 18 points to 8. A comfortable 16-2 victory over Wakefield at Knowsley Road earned Saints a third round trip to second division Halifax, who made the visitors work hard for a 24-16 victory. Widnes were favourites to win the semi-final at Wigan, but Saints produced their best performance of the season to win by 19 points to 2 in front of just over 16,000 spectators.

Wigan were clear favourites to win the final. They had already secured the first division title and had easily won the previous three Challenge Cup finals by margins of 20, 27 and 22 points respectively.

However, many of their players carried injuries into the final, including Ellery Hanley's torn thigh muscle. Saints were determined to redeem themselves in the eyes of their supporters after the 0-27 debacle of 1989. Only four of the 1989 squad were in the starting thirteen: Phil Veivers, Paul Loughlin, Les Quirk and Shane Cooper with two others, Gary Connolly and Paul Groves, on the bench. In contrast ten of the Wigan squad had played in the 1989 final against Saints.

The game did not start well for Saints and within twelve minutes they were twelve points down. Botica kicked a penalty in the fifth minute and soon afterwards Phil Veivers lost the ball in a ferocious tackle that left him knocked out and prone on the ground whilst Wigan seized possession and worked the ball wide to Myers who went over for a try. Botica then scored in the other corner and converted his own try. Many Saints supporters feared the worst as memories of 1989 came flooding back. However, to their great credit Saints players dug deep and limited Wigan to just a single point in the remaining 68 minutes.

Gregory's drop goal early in the second half stretched Wigan's lead to 13 points but just after the hour mark Wigan lost possession near their own line and smart handling gave Alan Hunte enough space to touch down in the corner. Paul Bishop landed a superb conversion and Saints were right back in the contest. A penalty goal nine minutes from time narrowed the gap to five points but Saints spilled too much ball to seriously trouble a tired Wigan side that held on for a 13-8 victory and a record fourth successive Challenge Cup triumph.

It was not a classic final but the players had given their all and although they were disappointed by the result, Saints fans were far less critical of their team than two years previously. Nonetheless it was Saints' fourth successive Wembley defeat and fifteen years had passed since a Saints skipper had last held the trophy aloft.

SAINTS 8 - WIGAN 13

Man of the match: Denis Betts

FINAL FACT

This was the fourth of Wigan's eight successive Challenge Cup final victories between 1988 and 1995.
The five point margin was the narrowest of the eight.

1996 CHALLENGE CUP FINAL

SATURDAY 27 APRIL at WEMBLEY

SAINTS v BRADFORD BULLS

SPONSOR: SILK CUT

SAINTS	BRADFORD BULLS
Steve PRESCOTT 2 *Tries*	Nathan GRAHAM
Danny ARNOLD 2 *Tries*	Paul COOK 6 *Goals*
Scott GIBBS	Matt CALLAND
Paul NEWLOVE	Paul LOUGHLIN
Anthony SULLIVAN	Jon SCALES *Try*
Karle HAMMOND	Graeme BRADLEY
Bobbie GOULDING (Capt) 4 *Goals*	Robbie PAUL (Capt) 3 *Tries*
Apollo PERELINI *Try*	Brian McDERMOTT
Keiron CUNNINGHAM *Try*	Bernard DWYER *Try*
Andy LEATHAM	Jon HAMER
Chris JOYNT	Jeremy DONOUGHER
Simon BOOTH *Try*	Sonny NICKLE
Andy NORTHEY	Simon KNOTT
Substitutes	Substitutes
Tommy MARTYN	Karl FAIRBANK
Ian PICKAVANCE *Try*	Paul MEDLEY
Vila MATAUTIA	Jason DONOHUE
Alan HUNTE	Carlos HASSAN
Coach: Shaun McRae	Coach: Brian Smith

Referee: Stuart Cummings

Attendance: 75,994

A revolution had taken place in Rugby League in 1996. Super League was launched and unprecedented amounts of money had started to flow into the game, enabling most Super League clubs to employ their players as full time professionals. The game was now a summer sport, with the 1996 season running from March to early September. The Challenge Cup was completed in the first two months of the season. Four substitutes were now allowed, with up to six changes permitted. Players were faster, fitter and fresher and rule changes had been implemented which meant the game was often played at a breath taking pace.

Saints, along with the other eleven Super League teams, entered the competition in the fourth round, joining twenty other teams in the draw. Saints received a tough looking away tie at Castleford, but breezed through 58-16 with Paul Newlove scoring a hat trick of tries. Their reward was a trip to Rochdale Hornets, where Saints won easily by 58 points to 20. Meanwhile, Salford had ended Wigan's eight year domination of the competition by surprisingly beating them at the Willows. Saints were drawn to visit Salford in round six and ran out 46-26 winners. Thus Saints had reached the semi-finals without playing at home and averaging 54 points a game!

13,424 spectators watched Saints defeat Widnes 24-14 at Wigan in the semi-final, with Steve Prescott earning the man of the match award.

Saints were strong favourites to win the final and the hot weather at Wembley ideally suited their helter-skelter all action style of play. A whole generation of supporters had never witnessed a Saints Wembley triumph and expectations were high. The game proved to be an absolute classic with thirteen tries and numerous swings in fortune. Substitute Alan Hunte was Saints' only survivor from the defeated 1991 side. However, Paul Loughlin and Bernard Dwyer, who both played for Saints in 1991, were in the Bradford side.

Scott Gibbs created the opportunity for Steve Prescott to score the opening try after just three minutes and Prescott added a second a quarter of an hour later. However, Scales scored for Bradford and Cook's conversion and subsequent penalty pulled the Bulls level at 8-8. Danny Arnold finished strongly putting Saints ahead but once again Bobbie Goulding could not add the conversion and when Paul squeezed over and Cook converted Bradford led 14-12 at half time.

The first 13 minutes of the second half were a disaster for Saints as first old boy Dwyer ploughed over for a try and then Paul scored his second. Two conversions put the Bulls 26-12 ahead and no side had ever won a final facing such a deficit. What followed was arguably the most unbelievable six minutes in Saints' Challenge Cup history. Three towering kicks from Goulding all resulted in tries for Saints, with Graham, the Bulls' full back, unable to deal effectively with any of them. Keiron Cunningham, Simon Booth and Ian Pickavance all touched down and Goulding converted all three scores to put Saints 30-26 ahead. Soon afterwards Arnold added another but Paul's superb hat trick try and Cook's conversion closed the gap to just two points with ten minutes left to play.

With Saints fans' nerves stretched to breaking point Goulding sent Perelini over and converted to secure the most sensational victory in Challenge Cup history and bring the famous trophy home to St Helens for the first time in twenty years. Saints went on the win the inaugural Super League title and complete the double for only the second time in their history.

SAINTS 40 - BRADFORD BULLS 32

Man of the match: Robbie Paul

FINAL FACT

Robbie Paul was the first player to score a hat trick of tries in a Challenge Cup Final but still finished on the losing side.

Ian Pickavance touches down to score the third try from a Bobbie Goulding kick in just six sensational second half minutes in the 1996 Wembley final. During this period Saints went from being 12-26 down to leading by 30 points to 26.

Alan Hunte is lying on his back but still manages to watch the drama unfold. Vila Matautia and Paul Newlove look on whilst in the background Bobbie Goulding is just about to start celebrating. The despairing expressions on the Bulls players' faces show how cruel the game can sometimes be.
(© Copyright rlphotos.com)

Paul Newlove and Keiron Cunningham have both had roads named after them.
(© Copyright Ken Bold)

The 1997 Challenge Cup was sponsored by Silk Cut and the programme cover emphasised this.

1997 CHALLENGE CUP FINAL

SATURDAY 3 MAY at WEMBLEY

SAINTS v BRADFORD BULLS SPONSOR: SILK CUT

SAINTS	**BRADFORD BULLS**
Steve PRESCOTT	Stuart SPRUCE
Danny ARNOLD	Abi EKOKU
Andy HAIGH	Danny PEACOCK *Try*
Paul NEWLOVE	Paul LOUGHLIN *Try*
Anthony SULLIVAN *Try*	Paul COOK
Tommy MARTYN 2 *Tries*	Graeme BRADLEY
Bobbie GOULDING (Capt) 6 *Goals*	Robbie PAUL (Capt)
Apollo PERELINI	Brian McDERMOTT
Keiron CUNNINGHAM	James LOWES *Try*
Julian O'NEILL	Tahi REIHANA
Chris JOYNT *Try*	Sonny NICKLE
Derek McVEY	Bernard DWYER
Karle HAMMOND *Try*	Steve McNAMARA 3 *Goals*
Substitutes	Substitutes
Ian PICKAVANCE	Paul MEDLEY
Vila MATAUTIA	Matt CALLAND
Andy NORTHEY	Glen TOMLINSON *Try*
Chris MORLEY	Simon KNOX
Coach: Shaun McRae	Coach: Matthew Elliott

Referee: Stuart Cummings Attendance: 78,022

The Super League sides entered the draw in round four and Saints were paired with Wigan at Knowsley Road. Saints were reduced to twelve men when skipper Bobbie Goulding was dismissed for a high tackle just before half time. Saints' remaining twelve men battled to a memorable 26-12 victory. Goulding was handed a six match suspension and so missed the next three rounds but returned for the final. Saints coasted to a 54-8 home victory over Hull in round five before beating Keighley at Cougar

Park 24-0 in round six. Saints faced Salford in the semi-final at Wigan and stormed home by 50 points to 20 in front of 12,580 spectators.

The final matched the contestants of the previous year's classic against each other once again. Thirteen of the Saints squad had also represented the club in 1996, whilst ten of the Bulls had also featured in the 1996 final. Saints once again started as favourites and a capacity crowd gathered to watch the game, which was labelled the Centenary Challenge Cup final. The main event was preceded by the Silk Cut Plate final in which Hull KR easily defeated Hunslet Hawks 60-16. This competition was not a success and was never repeated.

Man of the match Tommy Martyn opened the scoring in eighth minute, touching down a Bobbie Goulding grubber kick. Three minutes later Peacock powered over in the corner to bring the Bulls level. Loughlin them stretched out a long left arm to intercept a Karle Hammond pass and cantered in for a try. McNamara's conversion put Bradford 10-4 ahead. However, Saints equalised when Martyn again raced onto another Goulding grubber and Bobbie converted. Just before the interval Hammond showed great strength to somehow touch down when surrounded by Bradford tacklers and Goulding's kick enabled Saints to go to the dressing room with a six point lead.

The first twenty minutes saw Saints power into a match winning twenty point lead. Chris Joynt scored Saints' fourth try when put through a gap by Martyn and then Anthony Sullivan was adjudged to have touched down a Goulding kick although replays showed that he had lost the ball. Goulding converted both tries and added a penalty goal to put Saints 30-10 up with only nineteen minutes left. Tomlinson was then given the benefit of the doubt as he attempted to touch down a Bradford kick. Another Goulding penalty completed Saints scoring and although Lowes added a late try for the Bulls, Saints won more comfortably than the final score line might suggest.

Goulding let Chris Joynt collect the trophy from the new Deputy Prime Minster, John Prescott, exactly a century after Saints had taken part in the first ever final. Whilst celebrating an excellent victory, some Saints supporters expressed sympathy for popular ex-Saint Paul Loughlin, who appeared in his fifth and last Challenge Cup final and had ended on the losing side on each occasion.

SAINTS 32 - BRADFORD BULLS 22

Man of the match: Tommy Martyn

FINAL FACT

St Helens under 11s played against a combined Batley and Dewsbury side as part of the pre match entertainment and included future stars James Roby and James Graham in their team.

2001 CHALLENGE CUP FINAL

SATURDAY 28 APRIL at TWICKENHAM, LONDON

SAINTS v BRADFORD BULLS

SPONSOR: SILK CUT

SAINTS	BRADFORD BULLS
Paul WELLENS	Michael WITHERS
Sean HOPPE	Tevita VAIKONA
Kevin IRO	Scott NAYLOR
Paul NEWLOVE	Shane RIGON
Anthony SULLIVAN	Leon PRYCE
Tommy MARTYN *Try DG*	Henry PAUL *3 Goals*
Sean LONG *2 Goals*	Robbie PAUL (Capt)
David FAIRLIE	Joe VAGANA
Keiron CUNNINGHAM *Try*	James LOWES
Peter SHIELS	Brian McDERMOTT
Chris JOYNT (Capt)	Daniel GARTNER
Sonny NICKLE	Jamie PEACOCK
Paul SCULTHORPE	Mike FORSHAW
Substitutes	Substitutes
Tim JONKERS	Paul DEACON
Vila MATAUTIA	Paul ANDERSON
Steve HALL	Lee GILMOUR
Anthony STEWARY	Stuart FIELDEN
Coach: Ian Millward	Coach: Brian Noble

Referee: Russell Smith

Attendance: 68,250

Saints were given a difficult tie at home to Wigan Warriors in round four and had to be at their best to secure a 22-8 victory. A trip to Whitehaven in round five seemed a much easier prospect and coach Ian Millward rested several players. However the Cumbrians proved to be tenacious opponents and Saints were relieved to come away with a 34-22 win. A comfortable 54-16 victory over Huddersfield Giants enabled Saints to meet Leeds Rhinos in the semi-final at the JJB in Wigan. Saints edged an epic contest 27-22.

Because Wembley was being redeveloped the Challenge Cup final went 'on the road' between 2000 and 2007. Finals were played at the national rugby union stadia of England, Wales and Scotland, something that would have been unthinkable before the professionalisation of union in 1995.

Bradford and Saints contested the final for the third time in six years, Saints having won both previous meetings. However, Bradford were the cup holders, having defeated Leeds at Murrayfield in 2000, and they had notched up an impressive 197 points in the previous four rounds, so a close encounter was expected. Saints had five players in their squad of seventeen who had also played against the Bulls in the 1996 and 1997 finals: Paul Newlove, Keiron Cunningham, Tommy Martyn, Vila Matuatia and Chris Joynt. Sonny Nickle had returned to Saints, having played in the 1996 and 1997 finals for Bradford. Only Robbie Paul and Brian McDermott played in all three Bradford v Saints finals for the Bulls.

Cup final day was peppered with very heavy showers and this adversely affected the spectacle. There was to be no repeat of the flamboyant high scoring finals of 1996 and 1997.

Saints' game plan was based on a kicking game which was designed to take advantage of the huge 'in goal' areas behind the try lines. The Bulls' centre Rigon was sin binned early in the game for a blatant obstruction on David Fairlie. Saints pressed hard and in the eleventh minute Sean Long's slide rule kick was touched down by Martyn, with Long converting. The Bulls scored a penalty goal but Saints continued to have the upper hand and another Long grubber kick was collected by Keiron Cunningham, who scored by the posts. Long converted and Saints' other first half score was a Martyn drop goal. Bradford scored a second penalty just before the hooter and so Saints went in at half time with a 13-4 lead.

During the interval the heavens opened and the second half was played in atrocious conditions which made open rugby very difficult so the game became rather dour, with defences dominating. Bradford narrowed the gap to seven points with another penalty goal but never seriously threatened to overhaul Saints.

Prime Minister Tony Blair presented the cup to Chris Joynt and the Lance Todd trophy to Sean Long. Long stated in his autobiography that when he was announced as the winner 'The words I'd repeated in my head since I was a little lad were being said for real. My skin was tingling and I could have cried; I was that chuffed.'

SAINTS 13 - BRADFORD BULLS 6

Man of the match: Sean Long

FINAL FACT

Bradford were the first team to fail to score a try in a Challenge Cup final in the twelve years since Saints' disastrous 0-27 defeat to Wigan in 1989.

2002 CHALLENGE CUP FINAL

SATURDAY 27 APRIL at MURRAYFIELD, EDINBURGH

SAINTS v WIGAN WARRIORS SPONSOR: KELLOGG'S NUTRI GRAIN

SAINTS	**WIGAN WARRIORS**
Paul WELLENS	Kris RADLINSKI
Anthony STEWART	Paul JOHNSON
Paul NEWLOVE	Gary CONNOLLY *Try*
Martin GLEESON *Try*	Jamie AINSCOUGH
Darren ALBERT *Try*	Brett DALLAS *Try*
Tommy MARTYN	Julian O'NEILL
Sean LONG	Adrian LAM *Try DG*
Darren BRITT	Terry O'CONNOR
Keiron CUNNINGHAM	Terry NEWTON
Peter SHIELS	Craig SMITH
Chris JOYNT (Capt)	Mick CASSIDY
Tim JONKERS	David FURNER
Paul SCULTHORPE *Try*	Andrew FARRELL (Capt) *4 Goals*
Substitutes	Substitutes
Mick HIGHAM	Brian CARNEY
John STANKEVITCH	David HODGSON
Sean HOPPE	Mark SMITH
Barry WARD	Ricky BIBEY
Coach: Ian Millward	Coach: Stuart Raper

Referee: Stuart Cummings Attendance: 62,140

Saints' Challenge Cup campaign started with an easy 40 points to 6 win at Oldham. Next, a trip to Warrington looked to be a tough draw but Saints cruised through 36-14. Saints' travels continued with a journey to Halifax and they were given a surprisingly hard game but came through 26-20 to earn a semi-final against Leeds Rhinos at the JJB stadium in Wigan. Saints were on top form and their 42-16 victory made them favourites for the final against the old enemy. It was the first time that Saints had played a Challenge Cup final outside England.

Eleven of the Saints squad had played in the previous year's Challenge Cup final side, including the half back pairing of Sean Long and Tommy Martyn. Wigan full back Kris Radlinski had spent four days in hospital prior to the final being fed on an intravenous drip. He was passed fit to play shortly before the kick off and his outstanding defensive performance was the crucial factor in Wigan's somewhat unexpected victory.

Saints almost went ahead after nine minutes but Radlinski knocked the ball out of Tim Jonkers' grasp as he looked certain to score. Soon afterwards Wigan took the lead when Dallas scored and Farrell converted. The game was less than a quarter of an hour old when the Warriors doubled their lead, Lam jinking over for a try and Farrell converting. However Saints soon hit back when Darren Albert outjumped the Wigan defence to score from a towering Sean Long kick. Three minutes later Keiron Cunningham thought he had scored under the posts but the video replay indicated that he had put the ball down on Radlinski's outstretched leg rather than on the Murrayfield turf. However, there was no doubt about Martin Gleeson's try ten minutes later, which pulled Saints back to 8-12. There were no further scores in the first half.

Saints started the second half strongly and flying winger Albert burst through but was stopped in his tracks by a copybook Radlinski tackle. In the 50th Paul Sculthorpe powered over from dummy half but the referee awarded a penalty to Wigan for an incorrect play the ball. This proved to be a watershed moment as a minute later Wigan opened up an 18-8 lead when ex-Saint Connolly finished off a break and Farrell once again converted. Ten minutes later Cunningham set up a try for Paul Sculthorpe but crucially Long was again unable to land the conversion. Both sides had scored three tries but whilst Farrell had converted all the Wigan scores, Long had missed all three of his conversion attempts. Lam landed a drop goal to open up a seven point lead with less than a quarter of an hour remaining. Wigan thwarted Saints' increasingly desperate attacks and as time ticked away Farrell extended their lead with a penalty goal.

Saints fans left disconsolately ruing that their team's inability to make the most of their scoring opportunities had enabled Wigan to win the cup.

SAINTS 12 - WIGAN WARRIORS 21

Man of the match: Kris Radlinski

FINAL FACT

Saints had four Australians in their squad of seventeen: Darren Albert, Darren Britt, Peter Shiels and Barry Ward.

2004 CHALLENGE CUP FINAL

SATURDAY 15 MAY at MILLENNIUM STADIUM, CARDIFF

SAINTS v WIGAN WARRIORS SPONSOR: POWERGEN

SAINTS	WIGAN WARRIORS
Paul WELLENS *Try*	Kris RADLINSKI
Ade GARDNER	David HODGSON
Martin GLEESON	Sean O'LOUGHLIN
Willie TALAU 2 *Tries*	Kevin BROWN
Darren ALBERT	Brett DALLAS 2 *Tries*
Jason HOOPER	Danny ORR
Sean LONG 6 *Goals*	Adrian LAM
Nick FOZZARD	Craig SMITH
Keiron CUNNINGHAM	Terry NEWTON *Try*
Keith MASON	Quentin PONGIA
Chris JOYNT (Capt)	Gareth HOCK
Lee GILMOUR *Try*	Danny TICKLE
Paul SCULTHORPE *Try*	Andrew FARRELL (Capt) 2 *Goals*
Substitutes	Substitutes
Mark EDMONDSON	Terry O'CONNOR
Ricky BIBEY	Mick CASSIDY
Jon WILKIN	Danny SCULTHORPE
Dom FEAUNATI	Stephen WILD
Coach: Ian Millward	Coach: Mike Gregory

Referee: Karl Kirkpatrick Attendance: 73,734

Saints were handed some very difficult ties in the 2004 Challenge Cup but rose to the occasion every time. Super League clubs joined the competition in the fourth round and Saints had to travel to Odsal to play cup holders Bradford Bulls. An excellent team performance enabled them to win easily by 30 points to 10. Over 13,000 saw Saints' 24-16 victory over Leeds Rhinos at Knowsley Round in round five. Saints then squeezed past Hull FC 31-26 at Knowsley Road to secure a semi-final against Huddersfield Giants. Saints supporters formed the majority of the 13,134 crowd at Warrington and they enjoyed the superb 46-6 win.

Two events cast dark clouds over the build up to the final. Sean Long and Martin Gleeson had bet on Bradford to beat a much weakened Saints side on Easter Monday and were awaiting their punishment; lengthy bans seemed inevitable. Meanwhile Wigan coach Mike Gregory was revealed to be suffering from a life threatening bacterial infection.

Only seven of the Saints squad had played in the disappointing defeat to Wigan at Murrayfield two years previously, whilst nine of the Wigan team remained. Ricky Bibey played for Wigan in 2002 and Saints in 2004 and so was the only player to get winners' medals in both games. Paul and Danny Sculthorpe were the first brothers to oppose each other in a Challenge Cup final since 1950.

Saints supporters were cautiously optimistic of a first victory over the old enemy in a Challenge Cup final since 1966, but memories of the defeats of 1989, 1991 and 2002 made them nervous rather than confident.

Saints opened the scoring after just three minutes. Jason Hooper tackled Radlinski as he was about to kick and the Wigan full back lost the ball. It was scooped up by Willie Talau. He then fed Lee Gilmour who touched down. Sean Long added an excellent conversion. Wigan equalised with a try from Newton, converted by Farrell. Brown then thought he had given Wigan the lead but the video referee spotted a knock on in the build-up. Long edged Saints ahead with a penalty goal before perfectly executing a weighted grubber kick which was touched down by Talau. Long's conversion opened up an eight point gap. However, Dallas scored in the corner to narrow the gap to just four points. Saints were relieved that Farrell's conversion hit the post and bounced away. Saints then scored their third try just before half time when Paul Wellens showed great strength to touch down when being tackled by Radlinkski and Hock. Long's simple conversion gave Saints a 20-10 lead at the break.

Ten minutes into the second half Brown attempted to off load to Dallas but the ball went to ground and Paul Sculthorpe collected it. Although he was tackled short of the line he linked with Long shortly afterwards to score. Long's conversion and subsequent penalty goal opened up an eighteen point lead. Brown put Dallas in for his second try with fifteen minutes remaining. However, with time ticking away Long collected his own chip kick and fed Gilmour who put Talau over for his second try. Man of the match Long added the conversion to complete the scoring.

Saints had gained revenge for their defeat against the Warriors in 2002. Sean Long considered it was probably the best game that he'd ever played. 'If I could have bottled how I'd felt, I'd be richer than Bill Gates,' he said.

SAINTS 32 - WIGAN WARRIORS 16

Man of the match: Sean Long

FINAL FACT
This is the only time Saints have won a Challenge Cup final that was not played in England.

2006 CHALLENGE CUP FINAL

SATURDAY 26 AUGUST at TWICKENHAM, LONDON

SAINTS v HUDDERSFIELD GIANTS

SPONSOR: POWERGEN

SAINTS	HUDDERSFIELD GIANTS
Paul WELLENS	Paul REILLY
Ade GARDNER	Martin ASPINWALL *Try*
Jamie LYON *Try and 7 Goals*	Chris NERO
Willie TALAU Try	Michael DE VERE 2 *Goals*
Francis MELI	Stuart DONLAN
Leon PRYCE	Chris THORMAN
Sean LONG *Try*	Robbie PAUL *Try*
Paul ANDERSON	Paul JACKSON
Keiron CUNNINGHAM	Brad DREW
Jason CAYLESS *Try*	Jim GANNON
Jon WILKIN 2 *Tries*	Eorl CRABTREE
Paul SCULTHORPE (Capt)	Andy RALEIGH
Jason HOOPER	Stephen WILD
Substitutes	Substitutes
Lee GILMOUR	Steve SNITCH
James ROBY	Stuart JONES
James GRAHAM	Paul SMITH
Maurie FA'ASAVALU *Try*	Wayne McDONALD
Coach: Daniel Anderson	Coach: Jon Sharp

Referee: Richard Silverwood

Attendance: 65,187

The Saints team of 2006 was arguably the finest in the club's history. They went on to win the League Leaders' shield and the Super League Grand Final and were voted the BBC sports team of the year.

They were utterly dominant in reaching the Challenge Cup final. They hammered Doncaster Lakers 56-6, Bradford Bulls 42-18 and Catalans Dragons 56-10 to reach the semi-final, all three ties being played at Knowsley Road. Hull KR were crushed 50-0 in the semi-final at Huddersfield. Saints scored an average of 51 points in the four games.

Saints were strong favourites to beat a Huddersfield side that had surprised many by getting to the final thanks to some favourable draws and a splendid win over Leeds Rhinos in the semi-final. The core of the Saints 2004 cup winning team was still in place and was augmented by some first class recruits such as Jamie Lyon and Jason Cayless. Young stars James Roby and James Graham formed part of a formidable replacement bench.

It had been hoped to play the final at Wembley but its redevelopment had taken longer than anticipated so Saints made their second visit to Twickenham instead. From 1895 to 2004 the Challenge Cup had been played in the spring, but in 2005 it had changed to being played over the summer, with the final at the end of August.

Underdogs Huddersfield started strongly and in the sixth minute Aspinwall finished a fine move and De Vere's touchline conversion put them 6-0 ahead. Saints levelled after 21 minutes when Willie Talau touched down and Jamie Lyon converted and then took the lead four minutes before the interval. Sean Long scored after good work from Lyon and Ade Gardner and Lyon's conversion secured a 12-6 half time lead.

Saints soon added to their lead when Jon Wilkin, sporting a bizarre looking bandage aimed at controlling the bleeding from his broken nose, scored a try and then Maurie Fa'asavalu touched down a James Roby Kick. Lyon's conversions opened up a 24-6 lead. Saints were now in dominant form and added further tries from Lyon and Wilkin. Paul scored a consolation try for the Giants but Saints had the last word when Jason Cayless went over and Lyon kicked his seventh goal from seven attempts.

Sean Long became the first player ever to win the Lance Todd trophy three times. Saints had obliterated all their opponents in their cup run, scoring 246 points in total and never scoring less than 42 points in any round. The winning margin of 30 points in the final was Saints' widest ever. Saints supporters knew they had witnessed something very special.

SAINTS 42 - HUDDERSFIELD GIANTS 12

Man of the match: Sean Long

FINAL FACT

Robbie Paul faced Saints in four Challenge Cup finals and scored a total of four tries but was on the losing side every time.

Maurie Fa'asavalu is about to touch down James Roby's grubber kick to score the try that took the game away from the Giants in 2006. Maurie was signed by Saints after impressing in the rugby union world cup for Samoa. He came on as a substitute against Huddersfield and his victory dance after the final whistle entertained the rest of the team and the thousands of Saints fans. He was somewhat controversially selected for Great Britain in 2007. He returned to rugby union in 2010.
(© Copyright rlphotos.com)

Cunningham Court is situated within the housing development which has been built on the site of Saints' old Knowsley Road ground. The court was named after Saints' long serving hooker Keiron Cunningham, who featured in seven Challenge Cup winning Saints sides.
As Cunningham Court is quite a large building I suspect that there is more than one resident.
(© Copyright Ken Bold)

The programme cover of the 2006 Challenge Cup Final which was played at Twickenham.

2007 CHALLENGE CUP FINAL

SATURDAY 25 AUGUST at WEMBLEY

SAINTS v CATALANS DRAGONS

SPONSOR: CARNEGIE

SAINTS	CATALANS DRAGONS
Paul WELLENS *Try*	Clint GREENSHIELDS
Ade GARDNER 2 *Tries*	Justin MURPHY *Try*
Matt GIDLEY	John WILSON
Willie TALAU	Sebastien RAGUIN
Francis MELI	Younes KHATTABI *Try*
Leon PRYCE	Adam MOGG
Sean LONG *5 Goals*	Stacey JONES (Capt)
Nick FOZZARD	Jerome GUISSET
Keiron CUNNINGHAM (Capt)	Luke QUIGLEY
Jason CAYLESS	Alex CHAN
Lee GILMOUR	Jason CROKER
Mike BENNETT	Cyril GOSSARD
Jon WILKIN	Gregory MOUNIS
Substitutes	Substitutes
James ROBY *Try*	Remi CASTY
James GRAHAM	David FERRIOL
Paul CLOUGH *Try*	Vincent DUPORT
Maurie FA'ASAVALU	Kane BENTLEY
Coach: Daniel Anderson	Coach: Mick Potter

Referee: Ashley Klein

Attendance: 84,241

Saints received home ties in all three rounds prior to the semi-final. Batley Bulldogs were thrashed 78-14 and then Rochdale Hornets were hammered 70-10. Warrington Wolves provided much stiffer opposition in the quarter final but Saints overcame a half time deficit to triumph by 25 points to 14. Just over 14,000 spectators gathered at Huddersfield to watch Saints score six tries in a 35-14 semi-final demolition of Bradford Bulls. Most supporters expected Saints to be playing Wigan in the first final at the redeveloped Wembley stadium, but Catalans Dragons beat the

Warriors 37-24 in the other semi-final to become the first side from outside England to feature in a Challenge Cup final.

Thirteen of the Saints squad had played in the previous year's final. The newcomers were Matt Gidley, Nick Fozzard, Mike Bennett and Paul Clough. Approximately half of the Dragons team were French born, with the other half from the Antipodes. Saints were strong favourites to win but almost all the neutrals in the capacity crowd supported the underdogs and helped create a carnival atmosphere in the stadium prior to kick off.

Catalans were determined not be rolled over by Saints and their defence was outstanding in the first half hour. Saints conceded five penalties in the first fifteen minutes and struggled to achieve their usual fluency. However, James Roby came off the bench to register the first score of the game in the 33rd minute, breaking five tackles in a jinking run to the line. Sean Long's conversion opened up a six point lead but the Dragons quickly hit back when Khattabi touched down in the corner. Just before the hooter Saints put together their best handling move of the half and Matt Gidley fed Ade Gardner who touched down in the corner and Long added an excellent conversion to enable Saints to lead 12-4 at half time.

Six minutes into the second half Saints were gifted a try when Paul Wellens seized on a Greenshields fumble to score under the posts and Long's conversion opened up a fourteen point gap. The game was as good as over when a few minutes later Paul Clough scored Saints' fourth try, even though Catalans replied with a long distance try from Murphy. Long kicked a penalty in the 67th minute and Ade Gardner's second try late on sealed what was ultimately a comfortable victory.

Losing captain Stacey Jones said 'We were just beaten by probably the best club team in the world.' Essentially it was a solid all round team performance that secured the win rather than individual brilliance. This was reflected in the fact that the Lance Todd trophy was shared between Paul Wellens and Leon Pryce.

SAINTS 30 - CATALANS DRAGONS 8

Joint Men of the match: Leon Pryce/Paul Wellens

FINAL FACT

Leon Pryce and Paul Wellens were the first pair of players from the same team to share the Lance Todd trophy.

2008 CHALLENGE CUP FINAL

SATURDAY 30 AUGUST at WEMBLEY

SAINTS v HULL FC

SPONSOR: CARNEGIE

SAINTS	HULL F.C.
Paul WELLENS	Todd BYRNE
Ade GARDNER	Matt SING
Matt GIDLEY *Try*	Graeme HORNE
Willie TALAU	Kirk YEAMAN 2 *Tries*
Francis MELI 2 *Tries*	Gareth RAYNOR *Try*
Leon PRYCE Try	Danny WASHBROOK
Sean LONG 4 *Goals*	Tommy LEE
Bryn HARGREAVES	Ewan DOWES
Keiron CUNNINGHAM (Capt)	Shaun BERRIGAN
James GRAHAM	Peter CUSACK
Jon Wilkin *Try*	Willie MANU
Chris FLANNERY	Danny TICKLE 2 *Goals*
Paul SCULTHORPE	Lee RADFORD (Capt)
Substitutes	Substitutes
Lee GILMOUR	Richard HORNE
James ROBY	Garreth CARVELL
Paul CLOUGH	Tom BRISCOE
Maurie FA'ASAVALAU	Jamie THACKRAY
Coach: Daniel Anderson	Coach: Richard Agar

Referee: Steve Ganson

Attendance: 82,821

Saints' 2008 Challenge Cup campaign started with a very easy 56-0 thumping of London Skolars at Knowsley Road. Warrington Wolves visited Knowsley Road in the next round. The game was played at breakneck pace and the lead see-sawed from one team to the other but Saints edged a breathless encounter 40-34. Saints faced Hull KR at New Craven Park in the quarter finals and a late Ade Gardner try proved a crucial factor in a 24 points to 18 victory. Almost 20,000 spectators packed Huddersfield's Galpharm stadium for the semi-final clash with Leeds Rhinos. James Graham was the star in a 26-16 victory.

Many thought that Hull should not have been at Wembley as they had twice played Jamie Thackray in earlier rounds despite him being ineligible. However, the RFL had decided not to eject them from the competition, choosing instead to fine them £100,000, £40,000 of which was suspended. Nonetheless, they were rank outsiders as they had a number of players missing due to injuries and started without any specialist half backs. Fourteen of the Saints squad had played in the victory over Catalans in 2007. Paul Sculthorpe, Bryn Hargreaves and Chris Flannery replaced Nick Fozzard, Jason Cayless and Mike Bennett.

Paul Sculthorpe dislocated his shoulder after just 58 seconds. This was his final act as a rugby league player and ended a magnificent career on a very sad note. Man of the match Paul Wellens put Matt Gidley over for a try after just seven minutes. When Francis Meli sprinted 80 metres to score a fine try in the 17th minute and Sean Long converted Saints appeared to be fully in charge. However there were no further points in the first half and so Saints led 10-0 at the interval.

Hull scored early in the second half when Yeaman intercepted a pass from Keiron Cunningham and hared 90 metres for a try which was converted by Tickle. This revitalised Hull and when Yeaman added a second try just after the hour Saints supporters became increasingly nervous, as Tickle's conversion put the Humberside team ahead. The roar was as much of relief as of celebration when Leon Pryce put Meli over for his second try, which Long converted. Jon Wilkin then charged down a kick from Washbrook and collected the ball to race under the posts and Saints were 22-12 ahead. With seven minutes left Raynor squeezed in at the corner but Tickle could not convert. Nonetheless Saints' lead was cut to six points and the match remained in the balance until Pryce strode across for Saints' fifth try to clinch a hard fought victory.

Saints had won three successive Challenge Cup finals for the first time in their history. It was a golden age which supporters hoped would never end. Sadly it did. Saints have not played in a Challenge Cup final since.

SAINTS 28 - HULL FC 16

Man of the match: Paul Wellens

FINAL FACT

Club legend Keiron Cunningham received his seventh and final Challenge Cup winner's medal after the game. His other successes were in 1996, 1997, 2001, 2004, 2006 and 2007.

SUPER LEAGUE GRAND FINALS

- The first Super League Grand Final was played in 1998
- In the first two seasons of Super League the champions were the team that finished top of the table and so no Grand Finals were played. Saints came top in 1996 and so were the first Super League champions. The format of the play-offs has varied considerably, with the number of participating clubs varying between four and eight. Higher placed teams have received preferential treatment regarding home advantage and in some seasons the top two or three teams were given a second chance if they lost their initial play-off game.
- Saints have played in 10 finals, winning five and losing five
- Saints' highest score is 29 v Wigan Warriors (2000)
- Opponents' highest score is 33 v Leeds Rhinos (2007)
- Saints' biggest margin of victory is 22 v Hull FC (2006)
- Saints' biggest margin of defeat is 27 v Leeds Rhinos (2007)
- The highest attendance at any Super League Grand Final in which Saints have played is 72,582 v Hull FC (2006)
- The lowest attendance at any Super League Grand Final in which Saints have played is 50,717 v Bradford Bulls (1999)
- All ten Grand Finals have been played at Old Trafford, Manchester
- Saints won their first four Grand Finals but lost their next five

Anthony Sullivan challenges for the ball following a high kick in the 1999 Super League Grand Final.

Anthony was the son of former Great Britain captain Clive. He was signed from Hull KR in 1991.
He was a great athlete and was one of the fastest players to play for Saints.
Anthony represented Wales at both league and union.
(© Copyright rlphotos.com)

1999 SUPER LEAGUE IV GRAND FINAL

SATURDAY 9 OCTOBER at OLD TRAFFORD, MANCHESTER

SAINTS v BRADFORD BULLS SPONSOR: JJB

SAINTS	**BRADFORD BULLS**
Paul ATCHESON	Stuart SPRUCE
Chris SMITH	Tevita VAIKONA
Kevin IRO *Try*	Scott NAYLOR
Paul NEWLOVE	Michael WITHERS
Anthony SULLIVAN	Leon PRYCE
Paul SCULTHORPE	Henry PAUL *Try and Goal*
Tommy MARTYN	Robbie PAUL
Apollo PERELINI	Paul ANDERSON
Keiron CUNNINGHAM	James LOWES
Julian O'NEILL	Stuart FLETCHER
Fereti TUILAGI	David BOYLE
Sonny NICKLE	Bernard DWYER
Chris JOYNT	Steve McNAMARA
Substitutes	Substitutes
Paul WELLENS	Paul DEACON
Sean LONG 2 *Goals*	Nathan McEVOY
Sean HOPPE	Mike FORSHAW
Via MATAUTIA	Brian McDERMOTT
Coach: Ellery Hanley	Coach: Matthew Elliott

Referee: Stuart Cummings (Widnes) Attendance: 50,717

Saints won the inaugural Super League in 1996 by finishing top of the table. There was no play-off series or Grand Final. However a play-off series leading to a Grand Final was introduced in 1998 and the following year Saints reached the final for the first time having finished the regular season in second place, five points behind leaders Bradford Bulls.

A top 5 play-off series determined the finalists. Saints romped to a 38-14 qualifying play-off victory over third placed Leeds Rhinos at Knowsley Road. They then travelled to Odsal for a qualifying semi-final against the Bulls and were thumped by 40 points to 4. This result put Bradford straight into the final but all was not lost as Saints still had the opportunity to get there via a final eliminator against fifth placed Castleford Tigers at Knowsley Road. Saints won 36-6 to qualify for the Grand Final.

Bradford started strongly and Robbie Paul almost scored in the seventh minute but was just denied. However, his brother Henry put the Bulls in front midway through the first half. He side stepped Sonny Nickle and raced up the field but Sonny amazingly managed to drag him down a few metres short. However, the players' momentum slid them across the slippery turf to the try-line and the score was given. The simple conversion put the Bulls 6-0 ahead. The introduction of Sean Long from the substitutes' bench had a positive effect on Saints' play and eight minutes from the interval he slotted over a penalty after Bradford were penalised for offside.

Only two minutes of the second half had passed when Leon Pryce ran fifty metres to touch down. However, referee Cummings asked video referee Dave Campbell to investigate the passing movement which led to the 'try' and he adjudged that Withers had got a fingertip to the ball and had therefore knocked on. In a rare Saints attack Paul Atcheson was just held up short and then Lowes went over for Bradford but his effort was denied by the video referee.

Fourteen minutes remained when Apollo Perelini created an opening and good work by Keiron Cunningham, Sean Long and Paul Atcheson created just enough space for Kevin Iro to crash over in the corner. Again Mr Cummings asked the video referee to adjudicate and after an agonising wait he awarded the try. Sean Long added a magnificent touch line conversion to put Saints ahead for the first time in the game.

Both sides had chances in the final thirteen minutes and Iro was denied a second try by the video referee but in the event it did not matter as Saints held on for victory, just a fortnight after their crushing defeat by the Bulls in the play-offs.

SAINTS 8 - BRADFORD BULLS 6

Man of the match: Henry Paul

FINAL FACT

Dave Campbell, the video referee who somewhat controversially disallowed Leon Pryce's try, was an ex-Saints player who scored eight tries in his seventeen appearances for the club.

2000 SUPER LEAGUE V GRAND FINAL

SATURDAY 14 OCTOBER at OLD TRAFFORD, MANCHESTER

SAINTS v WIGAN WARRIORS

SPONSOR: TETLEY'S

SAINTS	WIGAN WARRIORS
Paul WELLENS	Jason ROBINSON
Steve HALL	Brett DALLAS
Kevin IRO	Kris RADLINSKI
Sean HOPPE *Try*	Steve RENOUF
Anthony SULLIVAN	David HODGSON *Try*
Tommy MARTYN	Tony SMITH *Try*
Sean LONG *4 Goals*	Willie PETERS
Apollo PERELINI	Terry O'CONNOR
Keiron CUNNINGHAM	Terry NEWTON
Julian O'NEILL	Neil COWIE
Chris JOYNT (Capt) *2 Tries*	Mick CASSIDY
Tim JONKERS *Try*	Denis BETTS
Paul SCULTHORPE *DG*	Andy FARRELL (Capt) *Try, 2 Goals*
Substitutes	Substitutes
Fereti TUILAGI *Try*	Brady MALAM
Sonny NICKLE	Tony MESTROV
John STANKEVITCH	Chris CHESTER
Scott BARROW	Lee GILMOUR
Coach: Ian Millward	Coach: Frank Endacott

Referee: Russell Smith

Attendance: 58,132

Saints had finished second in the table, three points adrift of leaders Wigan. Saints' qualifying play-off against Bradford Bulls resulted in an epic 16-11 victory, courtesy of a try by Chris Joynt after the hooter had sounded following the legendary 'Wide to West' length of the field movement. Buoyed by this success Saints crushed the Warriors 54-16 the following week to reach the Grand Final. To their credit Wigan bounced back to defeat the Bulls 40-12 in the final eliminator to book their place at Old Trafford.

This was the third ever Grand Final and the concept continued to grow in popularity. The attendance exceeded the previous year's by over 7,000. Saints took the lead in the seventh minute when Sean Hoppe showed great strength to touch down under pressure from Robinson and Dallas. Sean Long missed the conversion- his only miss of the game. Wigan responded well and Farrell shrugged off defenders to cross for the equalising try but missed the relatively simple conversion.

Captain Chris Joynt powered over to put Saints in the lead and the conversion made it 10-4. A rare Paul Sculthorpe drop goal completed the first half scoring.

Ten minutes into the second half Man of Steel Long put Man of the Match Joynt through for his second try and Saints had a comfortable 17-4 lead. The Warriors were far from beaten though and first Hodgson and then Smith went over for tries. Farrell's conversions brought them back to within a point. Ten minutes remained when Tommy Martyn's wide pass was gathered by Fereti Tuilagi who touched down in the corner. Long's superb conversion put Saints seven points in front. As the clock wound down Wigan were denied by the video referee before Tim Jonkers rounded off a fine move seconds from the end. Long's conversion gave the score line a slightly flattering look but there was no doubt that Saints were worthy winners.

SAINTS 29 - WIGAN WARRIORS 16

Man of the match: Chris Joynt

The 2000 Grand Final programme cover.

FINAL FACT

This was Jason Robinson's final game of Rugby League. He switched to union and was a member of the rugby union world cup winning side of 2003.

Keiron Cunningham is tackled by a Wigan Warriors player during the 2000 Super League Grand Final whilst Kevin Iro watches on.

Keiron played in no less than eight Grand Finals between 1999 and 2010. He was on the winning side on the first four occasions but sadly was on the losing side for four consecutive years from 2007-2010.

Kevin was known as 'The Beast', probably because he terrified opposing three-quarters. He was 6 feet 3 inches tall and weighed almost 15 stones. He scored Saints' only try in the 1999 Grand Final.

(© Copyright rlphotos.com)

Robbie Paul and Paul Newlove featured on the cover of the 2002 Grand Final programme. Grand Final winners receive rings rather than medals.

2002 SUPER LEAGUE VII GRAND FINAL

SATURDAY 19 OCTOBER at OLD TRAFFORD, MANCHESTER

SAINTS v BRADFORD BULLS   SPONSOR: TETLEY'S

SAINTS	BRADFORD BULLS
Paul WELLENS	Michael WITHERS *Try*
Darren ALBERT	Tevita VAIKONA
Martin GLEESON *Try*	Scott NAYLOR *Try*
Paul NEWLOVE	Brandon COSTIN
Anthony STEWART	Lesley VAINIKOLO
Paul SCULTHORPE	Robbie PAUL *Try*
Sean LONG *Try, 3 Goals, DG*	Paul DEACON 3 *Goals*
Darren BRITT	Joe VAGANA
Keiron CUNNINGHAM	James LOWES
Barry WARD	Stuart FIELDEN
Tim JONKERS	Daniel GARTNER
Mike BENNETT *Try*	Jamie PEACOCK
Chris JOYNT (Capt)	Mike FORSHAW
Substitutes	Substitutes
Sean HOPPE	Leon PRYCE
Peter SHIELS	Paul ANDERSON
John STANKEVITCH	Lee GILMOUR
Mick HIGHAM	Brian McDERMOTT
Coach: Ian Millward	Coach: Brian Noble

Referee: Russell Smith   Attendance: 61,138

Saints and Bradford Bulls were the top two sides in the league in 2002, with Saints winning the League Leaders' shield thanks to a marginally better points difference. The Bulls went to Knowsley Road in the qualifying semi-final and edged a very exciting encounter by 28 points to 26. Saints had a second bite at the cherry the following weekend and in dreadful conditions beat Wigan Warriors by 24 points to 8.

The final has a good claim to being the most exciting Grand Final of all time and Saints' victory was shrouded in controversy.

In only the second minute Paul Wellens caught a boot in his face which fractured his cheekbone. Play continued as he lay on the ground and Bradford worked the ball wide and Naylor scored. Man of the match Deacon converted and then added a penalty as Saints were forced to regroup in Wellens' absence. Saints' first try was somewhat fortuitous. After Sean Long launched a high kick the ball broke free from Sean Hoppe as he was tackled and Mike Bennett picked up the loose ball and sauntered over unopposed. After an agonising wait video referee Gerry Kershaw awarded the try. Keiron Cunningham then put Long over after Costin lost the ball in the tackle and Long converted to put Saints ahead 12-8 after half an hour. There was no further scoring before the interval.

The Bulls started the second half strongly and within seven minutes had opened up a six point lead with tries from Paul and Withers and one Deacon conversion. Saints rallied and after Peter Shiels and Paul Sculthorpe were both stopped just short of the line the ball was moved swiftly to the right and Martin Gleeson crossed. Although Long missed the conversion he kicked a penalty soon afterwards to make things all square with a quarter of an hour remaining. With less than a minute left Long landed a drop goal to seemingly seal victory but there was to be one more twist. Saints regained possession from the kick off but as Chris Joynt lumbered forward he fell to the ground anticipating a tackle that never came, as Deacon backed away appealing for a voluntary tackle. Joynt regained his feet and Referee Russell Smith waved play on, much to the Bulls' annoyance and Saints registered their third Grand Final victory.

SAINTS 19 - BRADFORD BULLS 18

Man of the match: Paul Deacon

FINAL FACT

Saints and Bradford Bulls clashed in three Challenge Cup finals and two Grand Finals between 1996 and 2002. Saints won all five matches.

2006 SUPER LEAGUE XI GRAND FINAL

SATURDAY 14 OCTOBER at OLD TRAFFORD, MANCHESTER

SAINTS v HULL FC

SPONSOR: ENGAGE

SAINTS	HULL F.C.
Paul WELLENS	Motu TONY
Ade GARDNER *Try*	Shaun BRISCOE
Jamie LYON *3 Goals*	Sid DOMIC *Try*
Willie TALAU *Try*	Kirk YEAMAN
Francis MELI *Try*	Gareth RAYNOR
Leon PRYCE *Try*	Paul COOKE
Sean LONG (Capt)	Richard HORNE
Paul ANDERSON	Ewan DOWES
Keiron CUNNINGHAM *Try*	Richard SWAIN (Capt)
Jason CAYLESS	Garreth CARVELL
Lee GILMOUR	Shayne McMENEMY
Jon WILKIN	Lee RADFORD
Jason HOOPER	Danny WASHBROOK
Substitutes	Substitutes
James ROBY	Paul KING
James GRAHAM	Richard WHITING
Mike BENNETT	Graeme HORNE
Maurie FA'ASAVALAU	Scott WHEELDON
Coach: Daniel Anderson	Coach: Peter Sharp

Referee: Karl Kirkpatrick

Attendance: 72,582

The Saints team of 2006 was one of the finest in the club's history. Some would claim it was the best ever. They had already won the Challenge Cup and the League Leaders' Shield before defeating second placed Hull FC 12-8 in the qualifying semi-final to secure a fourth visit to the 'Theatre of Dreams.' Hull bounced back from defeat by Saints by beating Bradford Bulls 19-12 in the final eliminator.

Saints started as warm favourites, despite Paul Sculthorpe's absence due to a knee injury. However, Hull almost opened the scoring but a superb double tackle from Paul Wellens and Jamie Lyon just forced Raynor into touch before he could touch down. Francis Meli put Saints ahead when he snapped up Sean Long's chip but Hull responded with a try in the corner from Domic. With the score locked at 4-4 and half time approaching Leon Pryce broke through to score in the corner and Lyon's excellent conversion put Saints 10-4 up at the break.

Saints extended their lead when Willie Talau scored after good work from James Graham, James Roby and Jason Hooper. When Ade Gardner soared above Raynor to collect Long's towering kick and Lyon converted it looked like the contest was over. However, Hull continued to carve out chances and it took some epic defence, with Wellens to the fore, to keep them out. However, it was Saints who completed the scoring when Keiron Cunningham forced his way over and Lyon converted to make it 26-4.

Hull FC had played their part in a compelling match but Saints were not to be denied the domestic treble.

SAINTS 26 - HULL FC 4

Man of the match: Paul Wellens

The cover of the 2006 Grand Final programme captured the excitement of what many consider to be the sport's premier British event.

FINAL FACT

Victory in the Grand Final completed an outstanding season for Saints. They won all three trophies on offer and made a clean sweep at the Man of Steel awards. Paul Wellens was Man of Steel, James Graham was Young Player of the Year and Daniel Anderson was Coach of the Year. In December Saints won national recognition when they were voted BBC Team of the Year at the Sports Personality of the Year awards.

Coach Daniel Anderson is clearly delighted to hold the Super League trophy after the victory over Hull in the 2006 Grand Final.

Daniel was appointed coach in 2005 after Ian Millward's dismissal. Saints reached every available final during his three full seasons in charge. They won the Challenge Cup final in 2006, 2007 and 2008. They won the Grand Final in 2006, but lost to Leeds Rhinos in both 2007 and 2008. He was awarded the BBC Coach of the Year award in 2006. Sean Long appears to overcome with euphoria as he sinks to his knees.

Black seems to feature heavily on Grand Final programme covers, as demonstrated in 2008 and 2014.

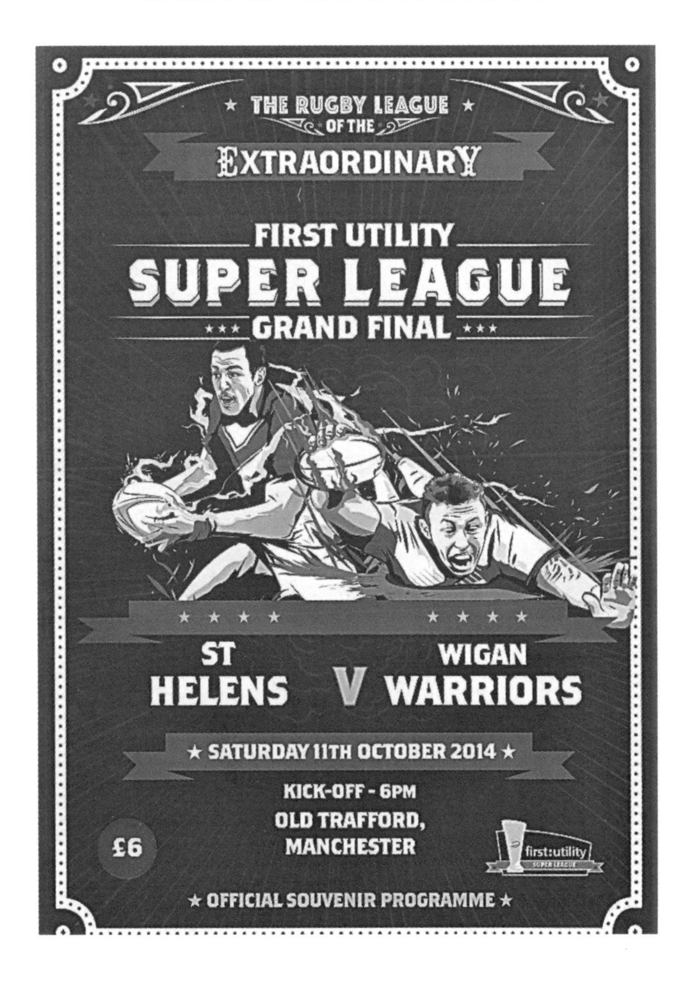

2007 SUPER LEAGUE XII GRAND FINAL

SATURDAY 13 OCTOBER at OLD TRAFFORD, MANCHESTER

SAINTS v LEEDS RHINOS

SPONSOR: ENGAGE

SAINTS	LEEDS RHINOS
Paul WELLENS	Brent WEBB *Try*
Ade GARDNER	Scott DONALD *Try*
Matt GIDLEY	Clinton TOOPI
Willie TALAU	Keith SENIOR
Francis MELI	Lee SMITH *Try*
Leon PRYCE	Danny McGUIRE
Sean LONG *Goal*	Rob BURROW *DG*
Nick FOZZARD	Kylie LEULUAI
Keiron CUNNINGHAM (Capt)	Matt DISKIN
Jason CAYLESS	Jamie PEACOCK
Lee GILMOUR	Jamie JONES-BUCHANAN *Try*
Chris FLANNERY	Gareth ELLIS
Jon WILKIN	Kevin SINFIELD (Capt) 6 *Goals*
Substitutes	Substitutes
James ROBY *Try*	Ali LAUITIITI *Try*
Mike BENNETT	Ryan BAILEY
James GRAHAM	Ian KIRKE
Maurie FA'ASAVALU	Carl ABLETT
Coach: Daniel Anderson	Coach: Tony Smith

Referee: Ashley Klein

Attendance: 71,352

Saints went into the final as clear favourites, as they had already won the World Club Challenge, the Challenge Cup and the League Leaders' Shield in 2007. They had beaten second placed Leeds 10-8 in a pulsating qualifying semi-final but the Rhinos had then crushed Wigan Warriors 36-6 in the final eliminator to reach Old Trafford.

Saints started strongly but Sean Long missed a relatively easy penalty kick. However, it was the Rhinos who took the lead with a Sinfield penalty after fifteen minutes. Five minutes later Leeds scored the game's first try through Webb and the conversion made it 8-0. Saints responded with an excellent try from James Roby, after good work from Long and Lee Gilmour. The simple conversion made it 6-8 and that is how it stayed until half time.

There had been nothing in a tight, compelling first half to suggest that either side would run away with the game after the interval, but that was what happened. After Saints had failed to turn pressure into points Lauitiiti bulldozed his way over and then Donald scored a superb try from well inside his own half. Sinfield's conversion put the Rhinos 18-6 ahead. Burrow popped over a drop goal and then Smith added to their lead when he collected a high kick from Sinfield to touch down. Sinfield's conversion and subsequent penalty pushed Leeds into a 27-6 lead and there was no way back for a tiring Saints team. Jones-Buchanan scored just before the end and Sinfield's conversion simply added to Saints' misery as what had been a marvellous season ended with a comprehensive defeat.

SAINTS 6 - LEEDS RHINOS 33

Man of the match: Rob Burrow

The 2007 club crests of Saints and Leeds Rhinos

FINAL FACT

This proved to be the first of three successive Grand Final defeats by the Rhinos, with a fourth occurring in 2011. Saints have played Leeds in eleven finals overall but have only defeated them three times.

2008 SUPER LEAGUE XIII GRAND FINAL

SATURDAY 4 OCTOBER at OLD TRAFFORD, MANCHESTER

SAINTS v LEEDS RHINOS

SPONSOR: ENGAGE

SAINTS	LEEDS RHINOS
Paul WELLENS	Lee SMITH *Try*
Ade GARDNER *Try*	Ryan HALL *Try*
Matt GIDLEY *Try*	Carl ABBLETT
Willie TALAU	Keith SENIOR
Francis MELI	Scott DONALD
Leon PRYCE	Danny McGUIRE 2 *Tries*
Sean LONG 2 *Goals*	Rob BURROW
Bryn HARGREAVES	Kylie LEULUAI
Keiron CUNNINGHAM (Capt)	Matt DISKIN
James GRAHAM *Try*	Jamie PEACOCK
Lee GILMOUR	Jamie JONES-BUCHANAN
Jon WILKIN	Gareth ELLIS
Chris FLANNERY	Kevin SINFIELD (Capt) *4 Goals*
Substitutes	Substitutes
Nick FOZZARD	Nick SCRUTON
Paul CLOUGH	Ali LAUITIITI
James ROBY	Ian KIRKE
Maurie FA'ASAVALU	Ryan BAILEY
Coach: Daniel Anderson	Coach: Brian McClennan

Referee: Ashley Klein

Attendance: 68,810

Saints had been soundly beaten by the Rhinos in the 2007 Grand Final but went into the 2008 re-match full of confidence and were strong favourites to win. They had already secured the Challenge Cup and the League Leaders' Shield and were looking to complete a clean sweep of domestic honours. Saints had easily beaten second placed Leeds 38-10 in the qualifying semi-final to secure a place at Old Trafford. The Rhinos defeated Wigan Warriors 18-14 the following weekend in the Final Eliminator to earn their place in the Grand Final.

Coach Daniel Anderson had decided to return home, so this was his final game in charge. The game was played in incessant rain, which did not suit Saints' freewheeling style of play. Nonetheless, they opened the scoring in the sixth minute when James Graham finished an excellent handling move to score to the right of the posts. Sean Long kicked the simple conversion. Man of the match Lee Smith scored in the 24th minute and Sinfield's conversion levelled things up. Shortly before half time Hall seemed hemmed in but grubber kicked past Willie Talau and won the race to touch down in the corner. Sinfield landed a superb conversion and so Leeds led 12-6 at the break.

Saints drew level just three minutes into the second half. A Sean Long kick was palmed back by Ade Gardner and Matt Gidley was on hand to touch down and Long kicked an excellent conversion. However a few minutes later Leeds regained the lead when McGuire touched down Sinfield's grubber kick, leaving his captain an easy conversion. Saints responded with an Ade Gardner try but this time Sean Long was unable to add the conversion. The Rhinos opened up an eight point lead in the 63rd minute when Francis Meli spilled a kick and McGuire danced over by the posts. Try as they might, Saints could not break down the Leeds defence again and the Rhinos held out to secure the victory. They had played the conditions much more effectively than Saints.

Unfortunately the Daniel Anderson era ended with a defeat but nonetheless he was one of the most successful Saints coaches ever. Paul Sculthorpe spoke very highly of him. 'Daniel's a truly great coach, his success rate speaks for itself. He's a very laid back guy most of the time, but you know that when he means business he means business. His defensive coaching has brought the club on so much during his time here.'

SAINTS 16 - LEEDS RHINOS 24

Man of the match: Lee Smith

FINAL FACT

In the match programme bookmakers William Hill made Saints 2/5 favourites to win the trophy. Leeds were 7/4.

2009 SUPER LEAGUE XIV GRAND FINAL

SATURDAY 10 OCTOBER at OLD TRAFFORD, MANCHESTER

SAINTS v LEEDS RHINOS

SPONSOR: ENGAGE

SAINTS	LEEDS RHINOS
Paul WELLENS	Brent WEBB
Ade GARDNER	Scott DONALD
Matt GIDLEY	Lee SMITH 2 *Tries*
Kyle EASTMOND *Try and 3 Goals*	Keith SENIOR
Francis MELI	Ryan HALL
Leon PRYCE	Danny McGUIRE
Sean LONG	Rob BURROW DG
James GRAHAM	Kylie LEULUAI
Keiron CUNNINGHAM (Capt)	Matt DISKIN *Try*
Tony PULETUA	Jamie PEACOCK
Chris FLANNERY	Jamie JONES-BUCHANAN
Jon WILKIN	Carl ABLETT
Lee GILMOUR	Kevin SINFIELD (Capt) *2 Goals, DG*
Substitutes	Substitutes
Bryn HARGREAVES	Ali LAUITIITI
Maurie FA'ASAVALU	Ryan BAILEY
James ROBY	Ian KIRKE
Lee GILMOUR	Luke BURGESS
Coach: Mick Potter	Coach: Brian McClennan

Referee: Steve Ganson

Attendance: 63,259

Saints and Leeds Rhinos contested the Grand Final for the third successive year. The Rhinos had won the previous two but Saints were determined to ensure that the result would be different this time around. Leeds had finished top and therefore won the League Leaders' Shield. Saints were three points behind in second place. Saints defeated third placed Huddersfield Giants 15-2 in the qualifying play-off and then beat Wigan Warriors 14-10 in an epic semi-final to book their place at Old Trafford. Leeds beat Hull KR (4th) 44-8 and Catalans Dragons (8th) 27-20 to qualify.

Remarkably, both sides had fifteen of the previous season's finalists in their squads of seventeen. Kyle Eastmond and Tony Puletua replaced Willie Talau and Nick Fozzard for Saints, whilst Brent Webb and Luke Burgess replaced Nick Scruton and Gareth Ellis for the Rhinos.

Saints opened the scoring in the fourteenth minute when Kyle Eastmond collected a ricochet from Jon Wilkin's kick to score and then converted his own try. A penalty goal put Saints 8-0 up and Saints supporters began to believe that it might just be their turn to celebrate. However, Saints' defence switched off to allow Diskin to scramble over from dummy half and when Francis Meli fumbled a kick Smith gratefully accepted the opportunity and touched down. The normally reliable Sinfield missed both conversions and the scores were level at 8-8 as the half time hooter sounded.

Sinfield put Leeds ahead for the first time when he landed a drop goal but Eastmond edged Saints back in front by kicking a penalty after a high tackle on Sean Long. Defences remained on top but Sinfield kicked a penalty to put Leeds 11-10 ahead. The game's crucial moment came seven minutes from time. Man of the match Sinfield threaded a kick through and Smith touched down from what appeared to most observers to be an offside position. However, to the dismay and astonishment of Saints players and supporters the video referee judged it to be a try and Sinfield's conversion put the Rhinos seven points up with time running out. Burrow added a late drop goal to seal a third consecutive Grand Final victory for the Rhinos over the Saints.

SAINTS 10 - LEEDS RHINOS 18

Man of the match: Kevin Sinfield

FINAL FACT

This was Sean Long's final game for Saints. He played in 265 matches over twelve seasons, scoring 124 tries, 812 goals and 20 drop goals.

2010 SUPER LEAGUE XV GRAND FINAL

SATURDAY 2 OCTOBER at OLD TRAFFORD, MANCHESTER

SAINTS v WIGAN WARRIORS

SPONSOR: ENGAGE

SAINTS	WIGAN WARRIORS
Paul WELLENS	Sam TOMKINS *Try*
Jamie FOSTER *Goal*	Darrell GOULDING *Try*
Matt GIDLEY	Martin GLEESON 2 *Tries*
Francis MELI *Try*	George CARMONT
Jonny LOMAX	Pat RICHARDS 2 *Goals*
Jon WILKIN	Paul DEACON
Matty SMITH	Thomas LEULUAI
James GRAHAM	Stuart FIELDEN
Keiron CUNNINGHAM (Capt)	Michael McILORUM
Bryn HARGREAVES	Andy COLEY
Iosia SOLIOLA	Harrison HANSEN
Chris FLANNERY	Joel TOMKINS
Tony PULETUA	Sean O'LOUGHLIN (Capt)
Substitutes	Substitutes
Paul CLOUGH	Mark RIDDELL Goal
James ROBY	Iafeta PALEA'AESINA
Andrew DIXON *Try*	Liam FARRELL
Jacob EMMITT	Paul PRESCOTT
Coach: Mick Potter	Coach: Michael McGuire

Referee: Richard Silverwood

Attendance: 71,526

2010 was Saints' final season at Knowsley Road and a victory over the old enemy at Old Trafford would have been the perfect way to mark the end of an era. After losing to Leeds Rhinos in the three previous finals, Saints supporters hoped that a change in opposition would lead to a change in fortunes. Sadly it would not.

Saints had finished the season in second place, four points behind leaders Wigan Warriors. They beat third placed Warrington Wolves 28-12 at home in the Qualifying Play-off before defeating

Huddersfield Giants 42-22 in the Qualifying semi-final in the last ever game at Knowsley Road. Fittingly, Keiron Cunningham scored the last ever try at the old ground.

Wigan lost 26-27 at home to Leeds Rhinos in the Qualifying Play-off. However, they comfortably defeated Hull KR 42-18 in the Preliminary semi-final before beating the Rhinos 26-6 at Headingley to book their place in the Grand Final.

An injury crisis had resulted in Saints recalling Matty Smith from his loan spell at Salford and he formed a makeshift half back pairing with Jon Wilkin.

The Warriors dominated the first quarter of the game and had established a sixteen point lead after twenty minutes. Ex-Saint Martin Gleeson scored two good tries and winger Goulding grabbed another. Pat Richards converted two of them. However, Saints belatedly began to settle into the game and in the 28th minute Andrew Dixon took an excellent pass from Jon Wilkin to score under the posts. Jamie Foster's conversion gave Saints a foothold in the game and completed the first half scoring.

Both sides came close to scoring in opening minutes of the second half but crucially it was Wigan that got the vital try after fifty-three minutes. Sam Tomkins showed great strength and agility to stretch a long arm out of a two man tackle to touch down. Although Riddell, who had taken over goal kicking duties following the departure of the injured Richards, missed the conversion, he subsequently kicked a penalty to put Wigan 22-6 ahead. Francis Meli scored a fine try in the corner with nine minutes remaining but Saints never seriously threatened to overhaul the Warriors, who were good value for their victory.

SAINTS 10 - WIGAN WARRIORS 22

Man of the match: Thomas Leuluai

Keiron Cunningham's statue, which is outside the entrance of Saints' stadium.
© Copyright Ken Bold

FINAL FACT

This was club legend Keiron Cunningham's final game. The one-club man played in 496 games for Saints and scored 175 tries.

2011 SUPER LEAGUE XVI GRAND FINAL

SATURDAY 8 OCTOBER at OLD TRAFFORD, MANCHESTER

SAINTS v LEEDS RHINOS

SPONSOR: ENGAGE

SAINTS	**LEEDS RHINOS**
Paul WELLENS (Capt)	Brent WEBB *Try*
Tom MAKINSON *Try*	Ben JONES-BISHOP
Michael SHENTON *Try*	Zak HARDAKER *Try*
Francis MELI	Carl ABLETT *Try*
Jamie FOSTER *4 Goals*	Ryan HALL *Try*
Lee GASKELL	Kevin SINFIELD (Capt) *6 Goals*
Jonny LOMAX	Danny McGUIRE
James GRAHAM (Capt)	Kylie LEULUAI
James ROBY	Danny BUDERUS
Tony PULETUA	Jamie PEACOCK
Jon WILKIN	Jamie JONES-BUCHANAN
Iosia SOLIOLA	Brett DELANEY
Paul CLOUGH	Chris CLARKSON
Substitutes	Substitutes
Andrew DIXON	Rob BURROW *Try*
Scott MOORE	Ryan BAILEY
Louie McCARTHY-SCARSBROOK	Ian KIRKE
Gary WHEELER	Ali LAUITIITI
Coach: Royce Simmons	Coach: Brian McDermott

Referee: Phil Bentham

Attendance: 69,107

2011 was a unique season for Saints as they had no ground of their own on which to play. Knowsley Road had closed and the site was in the process of becoming a housing estate, whilst Langtree Park was still under construction. Saints played all their 'home' fixtures at Widnes Vikings' Stobart Stadium. It was therefore no small achievement to finish in third place in the league table, seven points behind leaders Warrington Wolves.

Saints defeated Wigan Warriors 26-18 at the DW Stadium in the Qualifying Play-off and incredibly defeated them by exactly the same score at Widnes in the Qualifying semi-final. Leeds had only finished in fifth place but battled through to the final with victories over Hull FC, Huddersfield Giants and Warrington Wolves.

Coach Royce Simmons opted to play youngster Lee Gaskell at stand-off in preference to the experienced Leon Pryce. Saints had co-captains in Paul Wellens and James Graham but sadly neither would lift the trophy as Saints lost at Old Trafford for the fifth successive year.

The match was arguably the finest of the four Saints v Leeds Grand Finals, although the outcome was disappointingly similar to the previous three. Both sides started well in the wet conditions but defences were on top for the first thirty-four minutes. Jamie Foster and Kevin Sinfield had exchanged penalties before Rob Burrow set the game alight with a superb solo try from fifty metres out. Sinfield's simple conversion put the Rhinos 8-2 in front at the break.

Saints made an exceptionally strong start to the second half and forced the Rhinos to have four goal line drop outs and thought they had scored when Andrew Dixon appeared to have touched down a Jonny Lomax grubber kick but the video referee ruled a knock on. The breakthrough came when Tommy Makinson reached around Webb to touch down his own grubber kick and Foster's conversion levelled the scores. Five minutes later Saints took the lead when Michael Shenton finished off an excellent move. Jamie Foster missed the conversion but soon afterwards landed a penalty to put Saints 14-8 in front and added another from the centre spot after Sinfield put his restart kick dead.

Saints appeared to have all the momentum but things changed rapidly when Shenton left the field after injuring himself in a tackle. Paul Wellens had already retired with an injury and Saints' defence suddenly looked much more fragile. With fifteen minutes left Webb scored in the corner and Sinfield's excellent conversion cut the deficit to just two points and shortly afterwards he kicked a penalty to bring the sides level. With ten minutes remaining Burrow made a break and put Hall over to put the Rhinos ahead. The game was rapidly running away from Saints and Ablett's try, converted by Sinfield, opened up a ten point gap with only six minutes left. Hardaker completed the scoring with a late try which Sinfield converted to give the final score line a rather lopsided look. Leeds had scored 24 points in the final fifteen minutes to leave Saints shell shocked.

SAINTS 16 - LEEDS RHINOS 32

Man of the match: Rob Burrow

FINAL FACT

This was Saints sixth successive Grand Final and fifth consecutive defeat.

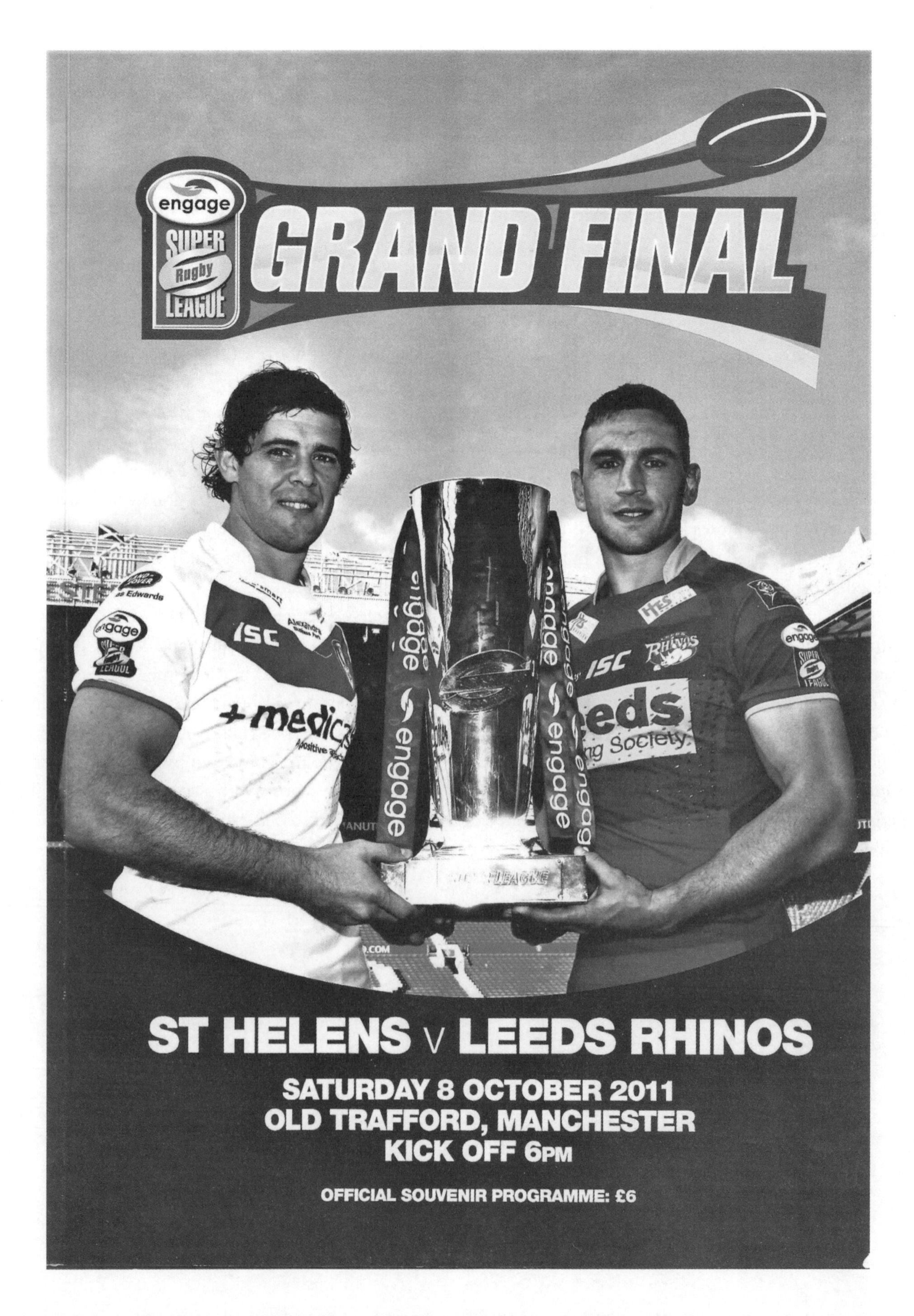

Paul Wellens and Kevin Sinfield hold the Super League trophy on the cover of the 2011 Grand Final programme.

This photograph wonderfully captures the delight and relief of the Saints players immediately after Tommy Makinson had scored the game breaking try against Wigan in the 2014 Grand Final.

James Roby slides in to congratulate Tommy whilst Kyle Amor and Louie McCarthy-Scarsbrook raise their arms in triumph as Jordan Turner rushes over to join in the celebrations. In contrast Matty Smith looks away, realising that Wigan's hopes of victory have almost gone.

(© Copyright rlphotos.com)

2014 SUPER LEAGUE XIX GRAND FINAL

SATURDAY 11 OCTOBER at OLD TRAFFORD, MANCHESTER

SAINTS v WIGAN WARRIORS

SPONSOR: FIRST UTILITY

SAINTS	WIGAN WARRIORS
Paul WELLENS (Capt)	Matt BOWEN
Tommy MAKINSON *Try*	Josh CHARNLEY
Mark PERCIVAL *3 Goals*	Anthony GELLING
Josh JONES	Dan SARGINSON
Adam SWIFT	Joe BURGESS *Try*
Mark FLANAGAN	Blake GREEN
Lance HOHAIA	Matty SMITH *Goal*
Kyle AMOR	Ben FLOWER
James ROBY	Sam POWELL
Mose MASOE	Dom CROSBY
Louie McCARTHY-SCARSBROOK	Joel TOMKINS
Iosia SOLIOLA *Try*	Liam FARRELL
Jordan TURNER	Sean O'LOUGHLIN (Capt)
Substitutes	Substitutes
Luke THOMPSON	Eddy PETTYBOURNE
Willie MANU	Tony CLUBB
Alex WALMSLEY	John BATEMAN
Greg RICHARDS	George WILLIAMS
Coach: Nathan Brown	Coach: Shaun Wane

Referee: Phil Bentham

Attendance: 70,102

Saints had won the League Leaders' Shield, despite losing their final two league games, as Castleford Tigers missed the chance to pip them at the post, losing in Perpignan against the Catalan Dragons on the final day of the regular season. Saints cruised through the play-offs, beating the Tigers 41-0 in the Qualifying play-off before defeating the Dragons 30-12 in the qualifying semi-final. Second placed Wigan beat Huddersfield Giants 57-4 and Warrington Wolves 16-12 to secure their place in the final.

Saints went into the final as underdogs as they had a number of key creative players missing through injury. These included Luke Walsh, Jonny Lomax, Jon Wilkin and Shannon McDonnell, so much was expected of Kiwi half back Lance Hohaia.

Wigan coach Shaun Wane promised 'It's going to be a full-on, rough and tough contest, there's no doubt about that.'

The opening two minutes of the match were brutal. Mose Masoe was penalised for a high shot in only the second tackle of the game. The Warriors gained good field position and a dangerous kick bobbled around close to the line before Ben Flower knocked on. The Wigan forward then punched Hohaia, knocking him to the ground. As the half back lay helpless Flower then punched him again. Referee Bentham dismissed Flower, who was subsequently suspended for six months. Lance Hohaia left the field and took no further part in the match. Thus Saints would have a one man advantage for almost the whole game but had no recognised half backs and had forward Louie McCarthy-Scarsbrook playing in the centres.

Smith gave Wigan the lead in the fourteenth minute by kicking a penalty after Saints were penalised for obstruction. Mark Percival evened things up with a penalty in the 29th minute but Saints' attacking play was disjointed and they struggled to make use of their numerical advantage. Wigan scored the game's first try with just nineteen seconds left on the clock before the interval when the ball was moved across quickly to winger Burgess, who squeezed over in the corner.

Saints finally managed to breach the Warriors' defence a quarter of an hour into the second half when Sia Soliola crashed over after taking James Roby's pass. Percival's simple conversion put Saints in front for the first time. Tommy Makinson was involved in two defining moments which determined the destination of the trophy. In the seventeenth minute of the half he hauled down Farrell when the Wigan player seemed certain to score and then with eleven minutes remaining he leapt above Smith and Bowen to collect Paul Wellen's bomb and twisted over to score the game breaking try. Mark Percival's conversion put Saints 14-6 ahead and despite a few scares in the final ten minutes Saints' excellent defence held out against numerous Wigan attacks.

After five successive Grand Final defeats between 2007 and 2011 Saints had at last given their supporters a night to savour at Old Trafford. Captain Paul Wellens, who had played in all five defeats, was able to really enjoy the moment as he held aloft the trophy to Saints' delighted supporters.

SAINTS 14 - WIGAN WARRIORS 6

Man of the match: James Roby

FINAL FACT

Ben Flower was the first ever player to be sent off in a Grand Final.

CHAMPIONSHIP FINALS

A top four play-off was first introduced in 1906/07 and continued to be contested until the brief introduction of two divisions in 1962/63. The semi-finals were 1v4 and 2v3 with the winners contesting the final at a neutral venue. The two division experiment only lasted for two seasons before a single championship was re-introduced. From 1964/65 until 1972/73 the top 16 clubs met in a seeded knock-out play-off competition to determine the finalists. The last Championship Final was contested in 1973 after which two divisions were re-introduced. Saints only won the First Division championship once, in 1974/75.

- Saints played in 9 Championship finals, winning six and losing three
- The 1967 final against Wakefield was drawn. Saints lost the replay
- Saints' highest score was 44 v Hunslet (1959)
- Opponents' highest score was 22 v Hunslet (1959)
- Saints' biggest margin of victory was 23 v Halifax (1966)
- Saints' biggest margin of defeat was 12 v Wakefield Trinity (1967 Replay)
- The highest attendance at any Championship Final in which Saints have played was 52,650 v Hunslet (1959).
- The lowest attendance at any Championship Final in which Saints have played was 19,386 v Huddersfield (1932)
- Five of the finals, including the 1967 replay, were played at Station Road, Swinton. The other venues were Odsal, Bradford (1959 and 1970), Belle Vue, Wakefield (1932), Maine Road, Manchester (1953) and Headingley, Leeds (1967)
- Saints' opponents were from Yorkshire in every final except in 1971 when Saints played Wigan

George Lewis was the very first Saints captain to receive the Championship trophy in 1932. His three successful goal kicks were crucial contributions to victory over Huddersfield in a tight game.
(© Copyright Saints Heritage Society)

The 1932 Saints squad are pictured with the Championship and Lancashire League trophies. This group were the most successful in Saints' history until the Jim Sullivan era. White shirts with a red band were Saints' favoured kit until the introduction of the red vee in the 1960s.
(© Copyright Saints Heritage Society)

1932 LEAGUE CHAMPIONSHIP FINAL

SATURDAY 7 MAY at BELLE VUE, WAKEFIELD

SAINTS v HUDDERSFIELD

SAINTS	HUDDERSFIELD
George LEWIS (Capt) 3 *Goals*	Len BOWKETT *DG*
Roy HARDGRAVE	Ernie MILLS
Bill MERCER	PARKER
Tom WINNARD *Try*	WALSHAW
Bob JONES	WALKER *Try*
Jack GARVEY	THOMPSON
Harry FRODSHAM	Gwyn RICHARDS
Bob ATKIN	RUDD
Dave COTTON	Cyril HALLIDAY
Ebor HILL	Herbert SHERWOOD
Ben HALFPENNY	Henry TIFFANY
Jack ARKWRIGHT	Thomas BANKS
Walter GROVES	Harold YOUNG

Referee: Mr F Fairhurst (Wigan) Attendance: 19,386

Saints had never reached the Championship final prior to 1932, although they had twice qualified for the top 4 play-offs. In 1927 they had finished in fourth position and travelled across town to play local rivals St Helens Recreation in the semi-final. The match was a chastening experience as Recs hammered Saints 33-0, only to lose in the final to Swinton. In 1930 Saints topped the table for the first time, but lost at home to fourth placed Leeds by 6 points to 10.

It was third time lucky in 1932. Saints finished in second place, just one point behind leaders Huddersfield. Once again Leeds visited Knowsley Road in the semi-final but this time Saints ground out a 9-0 victory in front of a crowd of 14,000 and earned the right to play Huddersfield, who had defeated Hunslet 12-9 in the other semi-final, in the final. The 19,386 spectators paid a total of just £943 to attend the match, which was held at Wakefield.

Saints had two star players, Alf Ellaby and Albert Fildes, missing as they were on their way to Australia as part of what proved to be an ashes winning squad. Huddersfield were without Stan Brogden for the same reason.

Saints won the toss and elected to play with the wind at their backs in the hope of gaining a lead which they could then defend in the second half. Tom Winnard missed two kickable penalties before Saints eventually managed to open the scoring with a converted try. Jack Garvey got the ball from a scrum and made a good break. He swerved around full back Bowkett and just as Tiffany made a cover tackle he passed the ball to Winnard, who touched down in the corner. George Lewis took over the kicking duties and landed a superb conversion. He then landed a penalty goal just before half time to put Saints 7-0 ahead at the break.

With the wind at their backs Huddersfield presented a much greater attacking threat in the second half. Bowkett kicked a drop goal to score their first points but soon afterwards Lewis restored Saints seven point advantage with a well struck penalty. Huddersfield scored a try after 65 minutes when Walker capitalised on confusion between George Lewis and Bob Jones. Both seemed uncertain what to do when the ball bounced loose and the Huddersfield man scooped it up and raced for the line. Winnard forced him out towards the corner flag and Bowkett missed the difficult conversion. Although Huddersfield applied considerable pressure in the final quarter of an hour the Saints defence held firm and when Mr Fairhurst blew the final whistle Saints were champions for the very first time in their history.

Unfortunately Saints were unable to build on this success. As the global economic crisis deepened money became increasingly scarce and good players were not replaced with those of similar quality. The following season Saints finished eleventh and from 1935 until 1947 Saints consistently finished in the bottom half of the table.

SAINTS 9 - HUDDERSFIELD 5

FINAL FACT
The average price of admission was less than one shilling (5p). The match programme cost one penny (0.4p)

1953 LEAGUE CHAMPIONSHIP FINAL

SATURDAY 9 MAY at MAINE RD, MANCHESTER

SAINTS v HALIFAX

SAINTS	HALIFAX
Glyn MOSES *Try*	Tyssul GRIFFITHS *4 Goals*
Steve LLEWELLYN	Brian VIEROD
Duggie GREENALL (Capt) *Try*	Tom LYNCH *Try*
Don GULLICK	Martin CREENEY
Stan McCORMICK	Terry COOK
Peter METCALFE *Try and 3 Goals*	Ken DEAN
John 'Todder' DICKENSON	Stan KEILTY
Alan PRESCOTT	Michael CONDON
Reg BLAKEMORE *2 Tries*	Alvin ACKERLEY (Capt)
George PARR	Jack WILKINSON *Try*
George PARSONS	Albert FEARNLEY
Bill BRETHERTON	Harry GREENWOOD
Ray CALE *Try*	Des CLARKSON
Coach: Jim Sullivan	Coach: Frank Dawson

Referee: Mr A. Hill (Dewsbury) Attendance: 51,083

The 1952/53 season marked Saints' transition from being a team that rarely contested for major honours to becoming one of Rugby League's most successful clubs. In 1951/52 Saints finished in twentieth position in a league of 31 clubs. In 1952/53 Saints only lost two of the thirty-six league games that they played and remained unbeaten in all eighteen away fixtures. However, they went into the Championship final having underperformed in both the Lancashire Cup final and the Challenge Cup final, losing to Leigh and Huddersfield respectively. The week after losing to Huddersfield at Wembley they hammered the same opponents 46-0 in the championship play-off semi-final and for the third time that season went into a final as strong favourites. Their opponents Halifax had finished in second place, six points behind Saints, and had squeezed past Bradford Northern 18-16 in the other semi-final

Over 51,000 spectators crowded into Manchester City's ground to see if Saints could replicate their outstanding league form in the final match of the season. Saints started strongly and after only four minutes a flowing move culminated with Steve Llewellyn sending Reg Blakemore over for a fine try which Peter Metcalfe converted. Metcalfe and Griffiths both kicked penalties before Duggie Greenall scored Saints' second try after Don Gullick had been stopped just short of the line. Metcalfe's conversion attempt hit the post and bounced away but Saints led 10-2. After twenty minutes Greenall put Metcalfe over for a try and although his conversion attempt once more bounced away off the post it seemed to many supporters that Saints already had the match in the bag as they had completely dominated the opening quarter. However, the programme notes described Halifax as ' a dour, fighting team' and they showed these qualities to haul themselves back into the game through another penalty goal and a rather soft try when Lynch darted over after taking a quick tap penalty. Saints went in 13-7 ahead at the break.

Griffiths soon kicked another penalty and Halifax almost took the lead when Lynch fly kicked a loose ball but with a clear run to the line in front of him he knocked on when attempting to gather the ball. This proved to be a decisive moment as Saints re-imposed themselves when firstly Ray Cale and then Reg Blakemore scored tries, the latter converted by Metcalfe to put Saints 21-9 ahead. Glyn Moses then sealed victory with a good try. Wilkinson scored Halifax's third try just before the whistle and Griffiths' conversion completed the scoring.

Saints had won an entertaining game 24-14 and were crowned champions for only the second time in the club's history. Saints have only finished outside the top eight on one occasion since 1953, when they ended the 1961/62 campaign in ninth place.

SAINTS 24 - HALIFAX 14

FINAL FACT

Six of the Saints team were Welsh rugby union converts: Glyn Moses, Steve Llewellyn, Don Gullick, Reg Blakemore, George Parsons and Ray Cale.

1959 LEAGUE CHAMPIONSHIP FINAL

SATURDAY 16 MAY at ODSAL, BRADORD

SAINTS v HUNSLET

SAINTS	HUNSLET
Austin RHODES *10 Goals*	Billy LANGTON *5 Goals*
Tom VAN VOLLENHOVEN *3 Tries*	Ron COLIN
Duggie GREENALL	Jim STOCKDILL *Try*
Brian McGINN	Alan PREECE
Jan PRINSLOO *Try*	Willie WALKER
Wilf SMITH *Try*	Brian GABBITAS
Alex MURPHY *2 Tries*	Kevin DOYLE *Try*
Abe TERRY	Don HATFIELD
Tom McKINNEY	Sam SMITH
Alan PRESCOTT	Ken EYRE
Brian BRIGGS	Harry POOLE *Try*
Dick HUDDART *Try*	Geoff GUNNEY *Try*
Vince KARALIUS	Brian SHAW
Coach: Jim Sullivan	Coach: Jack Walkington

Referee: Mr G. Wilson (Dewsbury) Attendance: 52,560

Saints finished the 1958/59 season at the top of the league table, winning 31 and drawing one of their 38 matches. They became the first ever side to score more than 1,000 points in a season. Saints were six points clear of their opponents in the Championship final, third placed Hunslet. Saints hammered 4th placed Oldham 42-4 at Knowsley Road in their semi-final play-off, whilst Hunslet shocked Wigan by winning 22-11 at Central Park in the other semi-final.

Despite their dominance in their league, Saints went into the final without a trophy in the cabinet. Wigan had won the Challenge Cup and the Lancashire League, whilst Oldham had beaten Saints in the Lancashire Cup final. Although Saints went into the match as strong favourites, their supporters were nervous, as some felt that the side had not performed to its potential in key games.

These fears were heightened during the opening quarter of the game. Although Austin Rhodes landed an early penalty goal, Hunslet responded with a try from Stockdill. Langton converted and by doing so ensured that he had played and kicked a goal in every one of Hunslet's 45 games during the season. Rhodes kicked another penalty but Doyle crossed for Hunslet's second try which was again converted. Saints found themselves 4-12 behind after seventeen minutes when the reliable Langton slotted over a penalty. Saints were struggling to find any rhythm and the eager Hunslet defence was easily coping with Saints misfiring attacks.

After 25 minutes Saints won the ball from a scrum inside their own 25 yard line. The ball was shipped out to Duggie Greenall who passed to Tom Van Vollenhoven. The South African seemed hemmed in but somehow eluded winger Walker before breaking through Langton's tackle. The Hunslet cover defence looked certain to stop him but he demonstrated great pace and agility to elude several tackles and used a strong hand off to push away other defenders on a pulsating dash to the line to score one of the finest tries ever witnessed in a Championship final. Rhodes' conversion made it 9-12 and Saints then embarked on a stupendous display of attacking rugby entirely out of keeping with the previous 25 minutes.

Rhodes kicked a penalty and then Vince Karalius set up a try for Alex Murphy, which Rhodes converted. Jan Prinsloo squeezed over in the corner after 35 minutes and Vollenhoven cut inside to score his second try just before the half time whistle. Austin Rhodes' conversion meant that in just a quarter an hour Saints had turned an eight point deficit into a twelve point advantage.

Six minutes after the break Vollenhoven completed his hat trick and soon afterwards Wilf Smith's converted try put Saints 32-12 ahead and the contest was over. Gunney and Poole did manage to score tries for Hunslet, but these were cancelled out by tries from Alex Murphy and Dick Huddart. The game had been a feast of entertainment on a scorching afternoon. Saints had scored the record number of points by any side in a League Championship final, whilst Hunslet's score of 22 was a record for any losing team. Austin Rhodes' ten goals were also a record.

SAINTS 44 - HUNSLET 22

FINAL FACT

All fourteen backs were less than six feet in height. Hunslet's Jim Stockdill was the tallest at 5ft 11½in, whilst scrum half Doyle was only 5ft 3½in tall.
Jan Prinsloo (5ft 11in) was Saints tallest player.

1965 LEAGUE CHAMPIONSHIP FINAL

SATURDAY 22 MAY at STATION ROAD, SWINTON

SAINTS v HALIFAX

SAINTS	HALIFAX
Frank BARROW	Ron JAMES 3 *Goals*
Peter HARVEY	Duncan JACKSON *Try*
Tom VAN VOLLENHOVEN	John BURNETT (Capt) 2 *Tries*
Keith NORTHEY	Alan KELLETT
Len KILLEEN *Try and 2 Goals*	Johnny FREEMAN
Alex MURPHY (Capt)	Barry ROBINSON
Wilf SMITH	Paul DALEY
John TEMBEY	Ken ROBERTS
Bob DAGNALL	David HARRISON
Cliff WATSON	Jack SCROBY
Ray FRENCH	Terry FOGERTY
John MANTLE	Colin DIXON
Doug LAUGHTON	Charlie RENILSON
Substitutes	Substitutes
Kel COSLETT	Brian TODD
John WARLOW	Hugh DUFFY
Coach: Joe Coan	Coach: Albert Fearnley

Referee: Mr D. S. Brown (Dewsbury) Attendance: 20,786

Rugby League abandoned its experiment of having two divisions after just two seasons and reverted to a single league comprising all thirty member clubs in the 1964/65 season. However, the play-off series for the Championship was extended to include the top sixteen clubs, rather than involving just the top four. The motivation was to make league fixtures more relevant for middle of the table sides.

Saints had an excellent season and finished top of the table, eleven points clear of Halifax who finished in seventh position. They were the first recipients of the newly established League Leaders' Trophy in recognition of this achievement. Saints were guaranteed home ties throughout the competition and beat sixteenth placed Barrow 23-7 in the first round and followed this up with a 24-6 defeat of eighth placed Hull KR in the second round. Fourth placed Wakefield Trinity visited Knowsley Road in the semi-final and provided stiff opposition before going down 10-5 to the Saints.

Saints were hot favourites to win the final. Halifax had exceeded most people's expectations by reaching the final from seventh place, having defeated Leeds (9th), Featherstone (15th) and Castleford (3rd). Saints started with their two star players, Tom Van Vollenhoven and Alex Murphy, not being picked in their preferred positions and perhaps as a result the backs did not play with their usual cohesion and style.

Halifax began well but both sides took few risks in the first twenty-five minutes. The Yorkshire side broke the deadlock when Daley snatched up a dropped ball and passed to captain Burnett who touched down. James converted to put Halifax 5-0 up. Saints rallied and Len Killeen kicked two penalty goals to reduce the deficit to one point at half time. However, ball handling prop forward John Tembey was injured before the interval and although he was replaced by John Warlow, Saints sorely missed his guile and leadership in the second half.

Burnett scored his second try, which was again converted by James, to put Halifax 10-4 ahead but Saints hit back with a Len Killeen try. However, he missed the conversion to leave Saints three points behind. Halifax continued to be much steadier in possession and Saints' attacks rarely troubled their defence. Saints supporters were disappointed rather than surprised when winger Jackson's try, converted once again by James, sealed victory for Halifax, who won the Championship for the first time since 1907.

Saints won three trophies in the 1964/65 season, the Lancashire Cup, Lancashire League and League Leaders' trophy, but the big two- the Championship and the Challenge Cup - had both eluded them as they were beaten in these competitions by Halifax and Wigan respectively. They were determined to remedy this the following season.

SAINTS 7 - HALIFAX 15

Man of match: Terry Fogerty

FINAL FACT

The attendance of 20,786 was the lowest Championship Final attendance since the Second World War. The only lower attendance in subsequent finals was 18,889 at the last ever final in 1973 between Dewsbury and Leeds at Bradford.

1966 LEAGUE CHAMPIONSHIP FINAL

SATURDAY 28 MAY at STATION ROAD, SWINTON

SAINTS v HALIFAX

SAINTS	HALIFAX
Frank BARROW	Barry COOPER *3 Goals*
Tony BARROW *Try*	David JONES
Alex MURPHY (Capt) *Goal*	John BURNETT (Capt)
Billy BENYON	Colin DIXON
Len KILLEEN *3 Tries and 6 Goals*	Johnny FREEMAN
Peter HARVEY	Barry ROBINSON
Tommy BISHOP	Gordon BAKER *Try*
Albert HALSALL *3 Tries*	Ken ROBERTS
Bill SAYER	David HARRISON
Cliff WATSON	Jack SCROBY
Ray FRENCH	Terry RAMSHAW
John WARLOW	Terry FOGERTY *Try*
John MANTLE	Charlie RENILSON
Substitutes	Substitutes
Bob PROSSER	Rodney EASTWOOD
Gerry HITCHIN	Hugh DUFFY
Coach: Joe Coan	Coach: Albert Fearnley

Referee: Mr J Manley (Warrington) Attendance: 30,634

The Championship final was the last game of a very successful season for Saints. They had comfortably defeated Wigan at Wembley the previous week to win the Challenge Cup for the third time in their history. They had finished top of the league table and were rewarded with the League Leaders' trophy and had also bagged the Lancashire League trophy. One last challenge remained; wresting the Championship trophy from holders Halifax, who had surprisingly beaten Saints 15-7 in the 1965 final.

As league leaders Saints had been guaranteed home games in the three previous rounds of the top 16 play-offs. They had easily defeated sixteenth placed Warrington 35-7 but ninth placed Oldham had provided stiffer opposition before going down 15-10. Saints beat Hull KR (12th) 14-6 in the semi-final to clinch a place in the final. Halifax, who only finished tenth, had beaten Bradford Northern (7th), Swinton (3rd) and Wigan (2nd), all away from home, to ensure that a repeat of the previous year's final would take place.

Only eight of the Saints squad of fifteen had played in the 1965 final- Frank Barrow, Alex Murphy, Len Killeen, Peter Harvey, Cliff Watson, Ray French, John Warlow and John Mantle. Eleven of the Halifax squad had featured in the previous year's fifteen. The attendance was over 10,000 more than that of the 1965 final, which demonstrated the high level of interest in what amounted to a re-match in most people's eyes.

Cooper opened the scoring with an early penalty goal but Saints took the lead after a quarter of an hour when Billy Benyon sent Len Killeen over for a try. Fogerty put Halifax in front again when he played the ball to himself and dived over for a try which Cooper converted. Albert Halsall scored after half an hour but Killeen's conversion attempt hit the post and bounced away. Soon afterwards Alex Murphy nudged Saints ahead 8-7 with a drop goal. After 35 minutes Halsall powered through a gap for his second try and this time Killeen made no mistake with the conversion. He then added a penalty goal to put Saints 15-7 up at the interval.

Albert Halsall became the unlikeliest of hat trick heroes when he stormed over for a crucial try four minutes into the second half. Len Killeen's conversion opened up a thirteen point gap. Tony Barrow extended Saints' lead with a good try in the corner and Len Killeen's second try, which he converted himself, meant the result was in little doubt with twenty minutes still to play. Killeen landed a penalty and scored a converted try to put Saints into an impregnable 35-7 lead. Halifax managed a late converted consolation try when Baker popped over the line but Saints fans were already celebrating a comprehensive victory which avenged the previous season's disappointment in the final.

Although Len Killeen registered twenty-one points, including a hat trick of tries, prop forward Albert Halsall's own hat trick merited the Harry Sunderland man of the match award.

SAINTS 35 - HALIFAX 12

Man of match: Albert Halsall

FINAL FACT

Saints won the Challenge Cup and the Championship double for the first time in their history in 1965/66.

Happy Saints supporters at the 1966 Championship final at Swinton.
(© Copyright St Helens Local History and Archives/ St Helens Reporter)

Len Killeen leaps to tackle a Halifax player. Len scored three tries and six goals in Saints' 35-12 victory (© Copyright. St Helens Local History and Archives/ St Helens Reporter)

1967 LEAGUE CHAMPIONSHIP FINAL

SATURDAY 6 MAY at HEADINGLEY, LEEDS

SAINTS v WAKEFIELD TRINITY

SAINTS	WAKEFIELD TRINITY
Frank BARROW	Gary COOPER
Tom Van VOLLENHOVEN	Ken HIRST
Tony BARROW	Ian BROOKE
Wilf SMITH	Neil FOX 2 *Goals*
Len KILLEEN 2 *Goals*	Gert COETZER
Peter DOUGLAS	Harold POYNTON
Tommy BISHOP	Ray OWEN Penalty *Try*
John WARLOW	John BATH
Bill SAYER	Bernard PRIOR
Cliff WATSON *Try*	Ted CAMPBELL
Ray FRENCH	Geoff CLARKSON
Brian HOGAN	Bob HAIGH
John MANTLE	Don FOX
Substitutes	Substitutes
Johnny HOUGHTON	David HAWLEY
Joe ROBINSON	Ken BATTY
Coach: Joe Coan	Coach: Ken Traill

Referee: Mr G. Philpott (Leeds) Attendance: 20,161

A momentous change to Rugby League rules took place during the 1966/67 season. Instead of one side having unlimited possession until it scored or made an error, a scrum was formed after four successive tackles had been made. The rule was trialled during the autumn and adopted as a permanent change in December- half way through the season! The programme notes declared that 'The new fourth tackle rule had been an unqualified success.'

Saints had finished fourth in the league table, eleven points behind leaders Leeds. They comfortably defeated 13th placed Leigh 34-12 at Knowsley Road in the first round of the top 16 playoffs and then defeated 5th placed Bradford Northern 15-8 in the second round to earn a semi-final against Castleford at Knowsley Road. The Yorkshire team were beaten 14-3 to earn Saints a place in the

Championship final for the third successive year. Six players, Frank Barrow, Len Killeen, John Warlow, Cliff Watson, Ray French and John Mantle played in all four matches, including the 1967 replay.

Opponents Wakefield Trinity had finished a place and seven points above Saints in the league table and were hoping to win the Championship trophy for the first time in their history.

The game was played in appalling conditions. It was extremely windy and there were very heavy rain showers interspersed with hail storms. Open rugby was impossible and the forwards dominated proceedings. Trinity opened the scoring in the tenth minute when Neil Fox landed a penalty goal. Saints responded with their best attacking period of the game. In the twentieth minute a clever pass from Ray French put Cliff Watson into just enough space for him to bulldoze through the Wakefield defence for a try which Len Killeen converted. The South African kicked a penalty a few minutes later which completed the first half scoring.

Tony Barrow thought he had scored a vital try when he collected a pass that had been meant for Brian Hogan and touched down in the corner. However, referee Mr Philpott adjudged that there had been a knock on, much to the dismay of Saints supporters. Trinity began to dominate field position and it took some heroic defence from Saints to keep the Yorkshire side at bay. However, Neil Fox reduced the gap to three points when he landed a penalty goal with eleven minutes left.

The pivotal incident of the game occurred with just six minutes remaining. Saints heeled the ball from a scrum near their own line but Tommy Bishop was unable to collect the slippery ball and Owen hacked the ball over the try line. Frank Barrow seemed to have the danger covered but Peter Douglas held back Owen as he chased the ball. Mr Philpott gave a penalty try, ignoring Barrow's pleas. The rule in place at the time meant that the conversion was taken from where the try would have been scored, rather than under the posts as is the case nowadays. Fox was unable to land the kick and so the scores were tied at 7-7. Fox had one final chance to win the game but missed a late penalty shot and the game ended in a draw.

SAINTS 7 - WAKEFIELD TRINITY 7

FINAL FACT

For the first time since 1930 the Rugby League Championship would have to be decided by a replay.

1967 LEAGUE CHAMPIONSHIP FINAL REPLAY

SATURDAY 6 MAY at STATION ROAD, SWINTON

SAINTS v WAKEFIELD TRINITY

SAINTS	WAKEFIELD TRINITY
Frank BARROW	Gary COOPER
Tom Van VOLLENHOVEN *Try*	Ken HIRST *Try*
Tony BARROW	Ian BROOKE 2 *Tries*
Wilf SMITH	Neil FOX 3 *Goals*
Len KILLEEN 2 *Goals*	Gert COETZER
Peter DOUGLAS	Harold POYNTON *Try*
Tommy BISHOP *DG*	Ray OWEN *Try*
John WARLOW	John BATH
Bill SAYER	Bernard PRIOR
Cliff WATSON	Ted CAMPBELL
Ray FRENCH	Geoff CLARKSON
Brian HOGAN	Bob HAIGH
John MANTLE	Don FOX
Substitutes	Substitutes
Johnny HOUGHTON	David HAWLEY
Joe ROBINSON	Ken BATTY
Coach: Joe Coan	Coach: Ken Traill

Referee: Mr J. Manley (Warrington) Attendance: 33,537

The contrast between the playing conditions at the original game and the replay could hardly have been greater. The howling wind and rain of the Saturday afternoon at Headingley were replaced the following Wednesday by a pleasant sunny spring evening at Swinton. 33,537 gathered to watch the game, over 13,000 more than attended the first game. Both sides were unchanged but Mr Manley replaced Mr Philpott as the match referee.

Trinity started strongly and Owen scored in the corner after nine minutes. Len Killeen landed a trademark long distance penalty after fifteen minutes to narrow the deficit to a single point but four minutes later Brooke scored Wakefield's second try to extend their lead to four points. Tommy Bishop popped over a drop goal in the 25th minute and Saints took the lead two minutes later when Tom Van Vollenhoven showed great skill to first beat Cooper and then to outpace Neil Fox to touch down for a splendid try. However, Saints' joy was short lived as Poynton scooted over just before half time and Fox converted to put Trinity 11-7 ahead at the interval.

Len Killeen kicked a penalty to lift Saints' hopes but just two minutes later Brookes scored his second try and Fox landed the conversion to put Wakefield 16-9 ahead. Hirst crossed for Trinity's fifth try and Fox landed a penalty to extend the lead to twelve points with twelve minutes left. Saints were shell shocked and were unable to respond and Wakefield secured their first ever championship victory.

Whilst many Saints supporters felt that their team could and should have won the original game, few could seriously argue that Wakefield were not good value for their win in the replay, especially as they outscored Saints by five tries to one. Ray Owen, whose penalty try had enabled Trinity to draw the original game, again proved to a thorn in Saints' side in the replay and deservedly won the Harry Sunderland trophy as man of the match.

SAINTS 9 - WAKEFIELD TRINITY 21

Man of the match: Ray Owen

The programme covers from the final and the replay

FINAL FACT

This was the first time Trinity had ever won the League Championship. They repeated the feat the following year, defeating Hull KR in the final.

1970 LEAGUE CHAMPIONSHIP FINAL

SATURDAY 16 MAY at ODSAL STADIUM, BRADFORD

SAINTS v LEEDS

SAINTS	LEEDS
Frank BARROW	John HOLMES 3 *Goals*
Les JONES	Alan SMITH *Try*
Billy BENYON	Sid HYNES
Johnny WALSH *Try and 2 DG*	Ron COWAN *Try*
Eric PRESCOTT *2 Tries*	John ATKINSON
Frank MYLER	Mick SHOEBOTTOM
Jeff HEATON	Barry SEABOURNE (Capt)
Albert HALSALL	John BURKE
Bill SAYER *Try*	Tony CROSBY
Cliff WATSON (Capt)	Albert EYRE
John MANTLE	Bill RAMSEY
Eric CHISNALL	Graham ECCLES
Kel COSLETT 4 *Goals*	Ray BATTEN
Substitutes	Substitutes
Alan WHITTLE	John LANGLEY
Graham REES	David HICK
Coach: Cliff Evans	Coach: Derek Turner

Referee: Mr W. Thompson (Huddersfield) Attendance: 26,358

Saints had finished the league season in third place, thirteen points behind league leaders Leeds. They beat 14th placed Warrington 36-8 in the first round of the top 16 play-offs and followed this up with a 16-5 home win over seventh placed Leigh to secure a semi-final at Wheldon Road against second placed Castleford. This was a rough, tough game which ended in a 9-9 draw. The tie was replayed at Knowsley Road and Saints triumphed by 21 points to 12 to reach the final.

Saints were very much the underdogs for the final. Leeds had won thirty of their thirty-four league fixtures and stormed to the final, scoring 116 points and conceding only 19 in their three play-off games.

Coach Cliff Evans sprang a surprise when he picked utility player Eric Prescott on the left wing rather than regular winger Frank Wilson.

Favourites Leeds took the lead in the seventh minute when Smith received a long pass and showed good pace to score the game's opening try. However, Saints took the lead with a converted try, hooker Bill Sayer touching down from an astute Frank Myler pass. Leeds regained the lead when Cowan scored a dazzling individual try, converted by Holmes. Kel Coslett's 23rd minute penalty proved to be the final score of an absorbing first half and Leeds led at the interval 8-7.

John Walsh edged Saints in front with a drop goal five minutes after the restart. Six minutes later Man of the Match Myler's sweetly timed reverse pass put surprise winger Eric Prescott in the clear and he raced away to score. Coslett's conversion attempt hit the post but Saints led 12-8 and another Walsh drop goal stretched Saints lead further before he forced his way over for the game clinching try. The heavens then opened and a tremendous downpour completely drenched the players and most of the spectators. Despite the awful conditions Coslett kicked two penalty goals to push Saints further ahead and Prescott added his second try five minutes from the end.

Captain Cliff Watson held the trophy aloft in front of thousands of very wet but delighted Saints supporters.

SAINTS 24 - LEEDS 12

Man of the match: Frank Myler

Frank Myler was one of Rugby League's greatest ever players. He played for Saints in 144 games and played over 500 games in total. A modern sports pavilion and recreation ground are named in his honour in his native town of Widnes.
(© Copyright Ken Bold)

FINAL FACT

Harry Sunderland trophy winner Frank Myler travelled to Australia soon after the game to captain the Great Britain touring side to Australia. He remains the last British player to lead an ashes winning team.

1971 LEAGUE CHAMPIONSHIP FINAL

SATURDAY 22 MAY at STATION ROAD, SWINTON

SAINTS v WIGAN

SAINTS	WIGAN
Geoff PIMBLETT	Colin TYRER *Goal*
Les JONES	Kevan O'LOUGHLIN
Billy BENYON *Try*	Bill FRANCIS
Johnny WALSH	Peter ROWE
Bob BLACKWOOD *Try*	Stuart WRIGHT
Alan WHITTLE	David HILL
Jeff HEATON	Warren AYRES
John STEPHENS	Brian HOGAN
Tony KARALIUS	Colin CLARKE
Graham REES	Geoff FLETCHER
John MANTLE	Bill ASHURST *Try and 2 DG*
Eric CHISNALL	Dave ROBINSON
Kel COSLETT (Capt) *4 Goals and DG*	Doug LAUGHTON (Capt)
Substitutes	Substitutes
Ken KELLY	David GANDY
Bobby WANBON	Eddie CUNNINGHAM
Coach: Jim Challinor	Coach: Eric Ashton

Referee: Mr E Lawrinson (Warrington) Attendance: 21,745

Saints had finished the league season in second place, two points behind leaders Wigan. Both sides were guaranteed home ties throughout the top 16 play-offs. Saints progress to the final was comfortable enough with victories over Huddersfield (15th) 28-5, Hull (8th) 30-5 and Leeds (3rd) 22-7. Wigan were given a surprisingly hard game by sixteenth placed Oldham but then recorded easy victories over Dewsbury (11th) and Wakefield Trinity (5th).

Saints were seeking to become league champions in successive seasons for the first time in their history. Nine of the squad, (Les Jones, Billy Benyon, Johnny Walsh, Alan Whittle, Jeff Heaton, Graham

Rees, John Mantle, Eric Chisnall and Kel Coslett) had played in the 1970 final victory over Leeds. Wigan included two ex-Saints players, Brian Hogan and Doug Laughton, in their pack.

Robinson opened the scoring with a try in the ninth minute to put Wigan ahead but the normally reliable Tyrer missed the conversion in addition to three other attempts at goal in the first half. In contrast Kel Coslett was in good kicking form and landed two penalties and drop goal to put Saints 6-3 ahead at the interval.

The second half was only a minute old when Ashurst dived over between the posts for a try which Tyrer converted to put Wigan ahead by 8 points to 6. Ashurst landed a drop goal in the 53rd minute to extend Wigan's lead to four points. With just under a quarter of an hour remaining John Mantle took exception to being roughly tackled and laid Ashurst out flat with a punch. Referee Lawrinson had no hesitation in sending him off. Man of the match Ashurst continued after treatment and soon landed another drop goal to leave Saints six points adrift and a man short with only nine minutes left. Saints started to throw the ball about in a desperate effort to break down the Wigan defence and got their reward when fine passing across the full width of the pitch created enough space for Bob Blackwood to touch down in the left hand corner. With less than five minutes remaining Coslett landed a superb conversion to cut the deficit to a single point.

With a minute left a Wigan attack broke down and the ball was snapped up by Saints. Johnny Walsh tried a drop goal attempt from fully forty yards out but Saints supporters groaned with despair as he sliced the ball well to the right of the posts. However, the ball bounced wickedly away from Wigan winger Wright and popped up into the arms of the injured Billy Benyon who touched down for the match winning try with Wigan supporters screaming that he was offside. Coslett's conversion was the final act of the game and Saints had truly snatched victory from the jaws of defeat. Lord Pilkington could hardly hide his delight when he presented the trophy to Saints skipper Kel Coslett.

SAINTS 16 - WIGAN 12

Man of the match: Bill Ashurst

FINAL FACT

This was the only time that old rivals Saints and Wigan played each other in a League Championship final. In fact it was the only occasion that Saints' Championship final opponents were from Lancashire.

1972 LEAGUE CHAMPIONSHIP FINAL

SATURDAY 20 MAY at STATION ROAD, SWINTON

SAINTS v LEEDS

SAINTS	LEEDS
Geoff PIMBLETT	John HOLMES
Les JONES	Alan SMITH
Billy BENYON	John LANGLEY
John WALSH *Goal*	Les DYL
Frank WILSON	John ATKINSON *Try*
Ken KELLY	Alan HARDISTY (Capt)
Jeff HEATON	David BARHAM
Graham REES	Terry CLAWSON 3 *Goals*
Les GREENALL *Try*	David WARD
John STEPHENS	Tony FISHER
John MANTLE	Phil COOKSON
Eric CHISNALL	Graham ECCLES
Kel COSLETT (Capt)	Ray BATTEN
Substitutes	Substitutes
Alan WHITTLE	David HICK
Kel EARL	Fred PICKUP
Coach: Jim Challinor	Coach: Derek Turner

Referee: Mr S. Shepherd (Oldham) Attendance: 24,055

Saints had beaten Leeds in the Challenge Cup final at Wembley the previous weekend and were hoping to win the Championship final for the third successive season. They had finished third in the league table, five points behind leaders Leeds. Saints first two ties in the top 16 play-off were both at Knowsley Road. They defeated Hull KR (14th) 25-5 and Rochdale Hornets (8th) 17-5. They had to travel to Odsal to play second placed Bradford Northern in the semi-final and just edged an exciting encounter by 14 points to 10. Leeds had beaten Leigh (16th), Widnes (11th) and Salford (5th) at Headingley in their run to the final.

The Saints team was unchanged from the successful Wembley side but Leeds made several changes. Hynes and Hepworth were both missing from the backs, replaced by Langley and Barham. Ramsay and Haigh were missing from the forwards. Their replacements were Ward and Eccles.

Saints supporters arrived at Station Road in high spirits after the previous week's triumph but a somewhat makeshift Leeds side were keen for revenge. Clawson, whose goal kicking had been erratic at Wembley, landed a penalty after ten minutes to settle his nerves. Eight minutes later Saints edged in front when Les Greenall dived over from dummy half after John Stephens had been tackled close to the line. Kel Coslett missed the conversion and there were no further scores in the first half.

The Leeds pack began to dominate proceedings, with Cookson and man of the match Clawson outstanding. Clawson landed a superb penalty from near the touchline ten minutes after the interval to edge Leeds ahead. The game's crucial action took place in the 63rd minute. Good quality handling created enough space for international winger Atkinson to squeeze over in the corner and a great conversion from Clawson put the Yorkshire side 9-3 ahead. John Walsh reduced the arrears with a towering drop goal from fully forty-five yards but Saints were unable to breach a well organised and committed Leeds defence in the remaining ten minutes and Leeds were worthy winners. Coach Jim Challinor said 'We were well beaten. We did not take the command which was there for us to take and we paid for it.'

SAINTS 5 - LEEDS 9

Man of the match: Terry Clawson

FINAL FACT

This was Saints last ever appearance in a Championship play-off final. The following season's final between Dewsbury and Leeds was the last one before the re-introduction of two divisions.

CLUB CHAMPIONSHIP FINAL

- This competition, which was the forerunner of the Premiership, only lasted for one season (1973/74). All clubs were awarded points for their performances over the season using a somewhat complex formula and the top sixteen clubs competed in the seeded knock-out competition.

- Warrington beat Saints 13-12 in the final, which was played at Central Park, Wigan in front of 18,556 spectators

- The programme included the following explanation of the 1974 Club Championship:

- To select the sixteen clubs to take part in this new competition, a system of merit points was introduced. At least three places in the 'top 16' were guaranteed for second division clubs by the playing of two preliminary rounds on a two-leg basis between the top twelve teams in the final Division Two table. The remaining places in the Competition proper were filled by the thirteen clubs which had gained the most merit points. Three merit points were awarded for winning a tie in a knock-out competition and points were also awarded for positions in the League table, the top team getting thirty points, the next twenty-nine and so on down to one point for the bottom of Division Two. Four points were subtracted for relegation, four points gained for promotion. The club with the higher number of merit points in any match has ground advantage.

THE NORTHERN RUGBY FOOTBALL LEAGUE

1974 CLUB CHAMPIONSHIP FINAL

St. Helens 12
v
Warrington 13

OFFICIAL SOUVENIR PROGRAMME — 10 p

This rather uninspiring drawing featured on the front cover of Championship Final programmes for at least fifteen years. It was used for the 1959 final v Hunslet and for every subsequent one up to and including the Club Championship final of 1974.
Over this period the price of the match programme quadrupled from 6d (2.5p) to 10p.

1974 CLUB CHAMPIONSHIP FINAL

SATURDAY 18 MAY 1974 at CENTRAL PARK, WIGAN

SAINTS v WARRINGTON

SAINTS	WARRINGTON
Geoff PIMBLETT	Derek WHITEHEAD 2 *Goals*
Dave BROWN	Mike PHILBIN *Try*
John WILLS	Derek NOONAN *Try*
Frank WILSON 2 *Tries*	Billy PICKUP
Roy MATHIAS	John BEVAN
David ECKERSLEY	Alan WHITTLE
Jeff HEATON	Alex MURPHY (Capt)
John MANTLE	Dave CHISNALL
Graham LIPTROT	Kevin ASHCROFT
Mick MURPHY	Brian BRADY *Try*
Eric CHISNALL	Bobby WANBON
George NICHOLLS	Ian MATHER
Kel COSLETT (Capt) 3 *Goals*	Barry PHILBIN
Substitutes	Substitutes
Alan GWILLIAM	John LOWE
John WARLOW	Wayne GASKELL
Coach: Jim Challinor	Player Coach: Alex Murphy

Referee: Mr P Geraghty (York) Attendance: 18,556

Two divisions were re-introduced in the 1973/74 season and since then a single league comprising all the professional clubs has ceased to exist. Even though the team that finished top of the first division, Salford, were crowned Champions, it was decided that an appetite remained for an end of season knock-out competition and thus the Club Championship was created. To select the sixteen clubs to take part a complicated system of merit points was introduced, with points earned for winning cup ties and also for final league positions. Warrington, who had already won the Challenge Cup, Players No. 6 trophy and the Captain Morgan trophy, finished top of the merit table despite only finishing fifth in the league table. Saints, who had finished the league season as runners up, came third in the merit table.

Saints defeated Workington Town 24-7 at Knowsley Road in the first round and earned another home tie against Castleford, which they won 25-9. They had to travel to Leeds in the semi-final and produced a fine performance to triumph 23-10.

The competition had failed to attract a great deal of interest amongst fans. A total of less than 12,500 attended the three Saints matches. However, a respectable crowd of well over 18,000 gathered at Central Park to witness the final game of a long, hard season. It was Saints 49th game and Warrington's 51st, a combined total of one hundred games!

Despite heavy rain, the two sides played out an exciting and entertaining game which was in the balance until the final whistle. Kel Coslett kicked an early penalty but Warrington registered the first try in the seventh minute when Mike Philbin accepted a good Murphy pass to score. Saints were back in front within minutes when Frank Wilson finished off an excellent break by Mick Murphy to score and Coslett converted. However, Warrington applied tremendous pressure on Saints' defence and Brady's try and Whitehead's conversion put Warrington 8-7 ahead in the 22nd minute. No further points were scored in the first half.

Warrington continued to dominate possession, winning thirteen of the game's twenty scrums. Despite this the Saints defence was not breached again until the 51st minute when Bevan's midfield run created enough space for Noonan to score. Whitehead's conversion opened up a six point gap. Saints responded well and with a quarter of an hour left Wilson scored his second try and Coslett's conversion meant that just one point separated the teams. Warrington tried a plethora of drop goal attempts to extend their lead but none succeeded. As the match entered its final minute Kel Coslett sent a towering forty yard drop goal attempt speeding towards Warrington's posts. However, the ball passed inches wide of the upright and the final whistle sounded. Warrington fans celebrated their fourth cup final victory of the season whilst Saints supporters were left to reflect on a trophy-less campaign.

SAINTS 12 - WARRINGTON 13

Man of the match: Barry Philbin

FINAL FACT

Although the Championship was decided simply by awarding the trophy to the side finishing top of the first division, the 1973/74 season was unique in having no less than seven cup finals, namely the Challenge Cup, Lancashire Cup, Yorkshire Cup, Players No. 6 Trophy, Captain Morgan Trophy, BBC2 Floodlit Trophy and the Club Championship. The Captain Morgan Trophy was not a success and only lasted for one season. The Club Championship was revamped and relaunched the following season as the Premiership Trophy, which continued until 1997.

PREMIERSHIP FINALS

The Premiership Trophy was an end of season seeded knock-out competition. It ran from 1975 until 1997. The top eight sides usually took part but on occasions the number of teams participating varied from as few as four (1996) to as many as sixteen (1975). There was no seeding in 1975.

- Saints played in 9 finals, winning four and losing five
- Saints' highest score was 36 v Hull KR (1985)
- Opponents' highest score was 48 v Wigan (1992)
- Saints' biggest margin of victory was 20 v Hull KR (1985)
- Saints' biggest margin of defeat was 32 v Wigan (1992)
- The highest attendance at any Premiership Final in which Saints have played was 36,598 v Wigan (1992)
- The lowest attendance at any Premiership Final in which Saints have played was 11,178 v Warrington (1977)
- Five of the finals were played at Old Trafford, Manchester. The other venues were Station Road, Swinton (1976 and 1977), Central Park, Wigan (1975) and Elland Road, Leeds (1985)

The cover of the first Premiership Final programme.

1975 PREMIERSHIP FINAL

SATURDAY 17 MAY at CENTRAL PARK, WIGAN

SAINTS v LEEDS

SAINTS	LEEDS
Geoff PIMBLETT	John HOLMES 2 *Goals*
Les JONES *Try*	Alan SMITH *Try*
Frank WILSON	Syd HYNES (Capt) *DG and Try*
Dave HULL	Les DYL
Roy MATHIAS *Try*	John ATKINSON 2 *Tries*
John WALSH	Mel MASON *Try*
Jeff HEATON *Try*	Keith HEPWORTH
John WARLOW	Roy DICKENSON
Tony KARALIUS	David WARD
John MANTLE	Steve PITCHFORD
Eric CHISNALL	Phil COOKSON
George NICHOLLS	Ray BATTEN
Kel COSLETT (Capt) *Goal*	Bob HAIGH
Substitutes	Substitutes
Ken GWILLIAM	Dave MARSHALL 3 *Goals*
Eddie CUNNINGHAM	Graham ECCLES
Coach: Eric Ashton	Coach: Roy Francis

Referee: Mr W Thompson (Huddersfield) Attendance: 14,531

Saints' league form had been superb throughout the 1974/75 season. They only lost three of their thirty fixtures and were crowned as Champions, finishing eleven points clear of second placed Wigan and fourteen ahead of Premiership final opponents Leeds.

This was the first ever Premiership competition. It was an end of season knock-out competition between the top twelve clubs from the first division and the top four teams from the second division. It was unseeded and so Saints gained no advantage from having finished top. They defeated Oldham 42-5 at home in the first round and required a replay in round two to beat Bradford Northern 14-5, following a 5-5 draw at Odsal. Saints overturned a 2-16 deficit to sensationally defeat Wigan 22-16 at Central Park in the semi-final and entered the final as favourites.

However, Leeds dominated the game and the warm, sunny conditions appeared to suit them more than Saints. Prop John Warlow left the field injured in the eighth minute and soon afterwards Holmes kicked a penalty to open the scoring. Three minutes later Mason side-stepped Geoff Pimblett and John Mantle and sped over for a try under the posts. Holmes' conversion opened up a seven point lead. Saints lost their other prop Mantle to injury after half an hour and so the pack needed a further reshuffle. The last five minutes of the half were a disaster for Saints. First Hynes dropped a goal and then he added a try which Marshall converted before Atkinson showed his speed and elusiveness to touch down to put his side 16-0 ahead at the interval.

Saints made a good start to the second half and were rewarded when Les Jones touched down in the corner and Kel Coslett landed an excellent conversion. However, Leeds scored another try through Smith and a penalty goal from Marshall restored their sixteen point advantage with just ten minutes remaining. Roy Mathias and Jeff Heaton scored unconverted tries before Atkinson ensured that Leeds had the last word with a long distance try and Marshall's conversion completed the scoring.

Saints may have been runaway first division Champions but their record in knockout competitions in 1974/75 had been woeful. They had lost in the first round of the Lancashire Cup, the first round of the Player's No. 6 trophy, the second round of the BBC2 Floodlit Trophy and the second round of the Challenge Cup. At least they had reached the final of the Premiership!

SAINTS 11 – LEEDS 26

Man of the match: Mel Mason

FINAL FACT

Saints appeared in the first Premiership final in 1975 and
also in the last one in 1997. They lost on both occasions.
Gate receipts were just £7,795 in 1975 and had risen to £359,303 in 1997.

1976 PREMIERSHIP FINAL

SATURDAY 22 MAY at STATION ROAD, SWINTON

SAINTS v SALFORD

SAINTS	SALFORD
Geoff PIMBLETT 3 *Goals*	David WATKINS 2 *DG*
Les JONES	Keith FIELDING
Peter GLYNN *Try*	Maurice RICHARDS
Derek NOONAN	Chris HESKETH (Capt)
Roy MATHIAS	Gordon GRAHAM
Billy BENYON	John BUTLER
Jeff HEATON	Steve NASH
John MANTLE	Mike COULMAN
Tony KARALIUS *Try*	Dean RAISTRICK
Mel JAMES	Bill SHEFFIELD
George NICHOLLS	John KNIGHTON
Eric CHISNALL *Try*	Colin DIXON
Kel COSLETT (Capt) *Goal*	Eric PRESCOTT
Substitutes	Substitutes
Ken GWILLIAM	Sam TURNBULL
Harry PINNER	Alan GRICE
Coach: Eric Ashton	Coach: Les Bettinson

Referee: Mr M Naughton (Widnes) Attendance: 18,082

The 1976 Premiership Final pitched the Challenge Cup winners (Saints) and the Champions (Salford) against each other. Fourth placed Saints defeated Wigan (5th) 19-6 at Knowsley Road in the first round of the top 8 play-offs. The semi-finals were played over two legs. Saints beat Leeds 12-5 at Headingley and 21-4 at Knowsley Road to cruise through 33-9 on aggregate. Salford had beaten eighth placed Hull KR and seventh placed Wakefield Trinity to reach the final.

This was Saints 51st match of a long, hard season. Nonetheless, supporters hoped the team could show the resolve demonstrated at Wembley a fortnight earlier to claim their third trophy of the season. Veteran Welsh forward John Mantle was playing his last ever game for Saints.

Despite the pleasant, warm conditions, during the first half neither side showed the flair that had enabled them to be the two finest teams in England over the previous nine months. The only score of an attritional forty minutes was a drop goal from Salford full back Watkins in the 30th minute.

Geoff Pimblett landed a penalty eleven minutes after the break to edge Saints ahead but soon afterwards Watkins landed his second drop goal to even things up at 2-2. That is how things remained until eleven minutes from time when Wembley hero Peter Glynn scored after good work from Roy Mathias and John Mantle to put Saints 5-2 ahead. With just two minutes remaining Eric Chisnall sealed victory by weaving around three defenders and touched down under the posts. There was just enough time remaining for Tony Karalius to score Saints' third try and for Geoff Pimblett to add the goal before Mick Naughton blew for full time.

The score line did not reflect the closeness of the contest but there was no doubt that Saints' performance had merited the victory.

SAINTS 15 – SALFORD 2

Man of the match: George Nicholls

FINAL FACT

Despite the fact that between them Saints and Salford have appeared in over a hundred finals, this remains the only time that they have met in a major final.

1977 PREMIERSHIP FINAL

SATURDAY 28 MAY at STATION ROAD, SWINTON

SAINTS v WARRINGTON

SAINTS	WARRINGTON
Geoff PIMBLETT *Try and 7 goals*	Derek FINNIGAN
Les JONES	Dennis CURLING
Billy BENYON (Capt) *Try*	John BEVAN
Eddie CUNNINGHAM *Try*	Steve HESFORD *4 Goals*
Roy MATHIAS *Try*	Mike KELLY
Peter GLYNN	Alan GWILLIAM *Try*
Ken GWILLIAM *Try*	Parry GORDON *Try*
Dave CHISNALL	David WEAVILL *Try*
Graham LIPTROT	Joe PRICE
Mel JAMES Try	Brian CASE
George NICHOLLS	Tommy MARTYN
Eric CHISNALL	Roy LESTER
Harry PINNER	Barry PHILBIN
Substitutes	Substitutes
Alan ASHTON	David CUNLIFFE
Tony KARALIUS	Mike PEERS
Coach: Eric Ashton	Coach: Alex Murphy

Referee: Mr G F Lindop (Wakefield)   Attendance: 11,178

Saints had finished the season as runners up in the league, five points behind Champions Featherstone Rovers. Saints played seventh placed Wigan at Knowsley Road in the first round and drew 10-10. Saints won the replay at Central Park 8-3. The semi-finals were played over two legs but Saints' tie against third placed Castleford was as good as over after the first leg, as Saints coasted to a 36-12 victory. Saints won the second leg 25-13 to record an aggregate victory of 61-25. Fifth placed Warrington's route to the final was extraordinary. They lost 18-13 at Hull KR in the first round but Rovers were subsequently disqualified for playing Phil Lowe against the RL council's instructions. They then lost the first leg of the semi-final 13-17 at Featherstone but won the second leg 11-1 to reach the final.

Just over 11,000 spectators gathered at Station Road in Swinton to watch the final. It was the lowest attendance at any of the twenty-three Premiership finals. The match was truly a game of two very different halves. The first half was intense and physical with just nine points scored. As the players tired in the second half defences became slacker and a fiesta of 43 more points was the result.

Geoff Pimblett opened the scoring in the twelfth minute with a penalty. However, almost half an hour had passed before the game's first try was scored by Alan Gwilliam and Hesford's conversion put Warrington 5-2 ahead. Pimblett then landed a second penalty and as a result Warrington led 5-4 at the break.

The second half was only three minutes old when Alan Gwilliam and Harry Pinner were involved in a punch up which resulted in referee Lindop sending both of them off. This seemed to galvanise Saints and within a couple of minutes Billy Benyon accepted a pass from Pimblett to scorch over for Saints' first try, which Geoff converted. Man of the match Pimblett then scored a try himself in the corner and landed a superb conversion. Although Eddie Cunningham had an effort disallowed as he was adjudged to have bounced the ball, Saints were now well on top and Roy Mathias added another try to put Saints 17-5 ahead. With a quarter of an hour remaining Philbin gave Warrington brief hope with a try but almost immediately Cunningham produced a fine burst to score from 40 metres out. Another Pimblett goal made it 22-10 and the game threatened to become a rout when first Ken Gwilliam and then Mel James scored converted tries. Warrington made the score a little more respectable with late tries from Gordon and Weavill and Hesford's conversions made the final score 32-20.

SAINTS 32 – WARRINGTON 20

Man of the match: Geoff Pimblett

FINAL FACT

Two pairs of brothers played in the final. Whilst Eric and Dave Chisnall both represented Saints, the Gwilliam brothers had divided loyalties. Ken scored a try for Saints and Alan scored one for Warrington before he was sent off.

1985 PREMIERSHIP FINAL

SATURDAY 17 MAY at ELLAND RD, LEEDS

SAINTS v HULL KINGSTON ROVERS   SPONSOR: SLALOM LAGER

SAINTS	HULL KR
Phil VEIVERS *Try*	George FAIRBURN *Try and 2 Goals*
Barry LEDGER 2 *Tries*	Garry CLARK
Steve PETERS	Ian ROBINSON *Try*
MAL MENINGA 2 *Tries*	Gary PROHM
Sean DAY 4 *Goals*	David LAWS *Try*
Chris ARKWRIGHT	Mike SMITH
Neil HOLDING	GORDON SMITH
Tony BURKE	Mark BROADHURST
Gary AINSWORTH *Try*	David WATKINSON (Capt)
Peter GORLEY	Asuquo EMA
Andy PLATT	Andy KELLY
Roy HEGGARTY	Phil HOGAN
Harry PINNER (Capt) *Try*	David HALL
Substitutes	Substitutes
Shaun ALLEN	Paul HARKIN
Paul FORBER	John LYDIAT
Coach: Billy Benyon	Coach: ROGER Millward

Referee: Stan Wall (Leigh)   Attendance: 15,518

The Premiership final featured the sides that finished first and second in the league. Hull KR were champions for the second successive season and Saints, inspired by superstar Mal Meninga, finished just three points adrift in second position. Saints easily beat seventh placed Widnes 26-2 in the first round and then crushed Wigan 37-14 in the semi-final. The final was played at Leeds United's ground. Saints had scored an average of over thirty points a game in the league season and the large pitch and dry conditions suited them perfectly.

Gary Ainsworth opened the scoring in the second minute with a good try but Fairburn dodged over from a scrum to bring Rovers level at 6-6. Phil Veivers did well to put Saints ahead when he touched down under pressure for Saints' second try. Barry Ledger used his speed to good effect to increase Saints' lead but Laws kept Hull KR in the game when he took Prohm's pass to score. Mal Meninga then intercepted Hall's pass and cantered forty metres to touch down. Robinson scored the seventh and final try of a frantic first half after good work from Broadhurst. Sean Day had kicked three goals and Fairburn one so Saints led 22-14 at the interval.

Both teams showed more defensive resilience in the opening twenty-three minutes of the second half and the only score came from a Fairburn penalty. As Rovers began to sense they had a real opportunity to draw level Mal Meninga turned the game on its head. He intercepted another Hall pass inside Saints' own 25 yard area and powered down the field. Fairburn and Clark gave chase but the Australian held them off to score a truly game-breaking try. Captain Pinner swerved in for Saints' sixth try in the 72nd minute before a late Ledger try completed the scoring.

Saints scored seven tries and Sean Day added four goals to score a then record 36 points in a Premiership final. As well as the trophy Saints received a cheque for £8,000 as winners. It was Mal Meninga's last game for Saints. Although he only played for a single season in the Red Vee, his legendary status in the club's history was guaranteed.

SAINTS 36 HULL KINGSTON ROVERS 16

Man of the match: Harry Pinner

FINAL FACT

This was Man of the Match Harry Pinner's 300th game for the club.

1988 PREMIERSHIP FINAL

SUNDAY 15 MAY at OLD TRAFFORD, MANCHESTER

SAINTS v WIDNES

SPONSOR: STONES BITTER

SAINTS	WIDNES
Paul LOUGHLIN 3 *Goals*	Duncan PLATT *Goal*
Barry LEDGER *Try*	Rick THACKRAY
David TANNER	Andy CURRIER 4 *Goals*
Mark ELIA	Darren WRIGHT 2 *Tries*
Les QUIRK	Martin OFFIAH
Mark BAILEY	Barry DOWD
Neil HOLDING	David HULME 2 *Tries*
Tony BURKE	Kurt SORENSEN (Capt) *Try*
Paul GROVES (Capt)	Phil McKENZIE *Try*
Stuart EVANS	Joe GRIMA
Paul FORBER	Mike O'NEILL
John FIELDHOUSE	Paul HULME
Roy HAGGERTY *Try*	Richard EYRES
Substitutes	Substitutes
Shaun ALLEN	Alan TAIT *Try*
Bernard DWYER	Steve O'NEILL
Coach: Alex Murphy	Coach: Doug Laughton

Referee: John Holdsworth (Kippax)

Attendance: 35,252

Saints had finished the league season in second place, four points behind champions Widnes. Saints brushed aside seventh placed Castleford by 40 points to 8 in the first round and defeated fourth placed Bradford Northern 24-10 in the semi-final to reach the final for the fifth time. However, it was their first visit to Old Trafford in a Premiership final. The move to Manchester United's stadium had proved to be a great success. The highest attendance at Saints' previous four finals had been just over 18,000 in 1976. Almost double that watched the 1988 final.

A sunny spring day set the stage for an open game. Saints started well enough and a Paul Loughlin penalty gave them an early lead but Sorensen bulldozed through Neil Holding to score the game's first try after eight minutes, which was converted by Currier. Widnes continually stretched the Saints defence and Wright and Hulme added further tries, one of which was converted, to leave Saints trailing 2-16 at the interval.

Loughlin landed his second penalty early in the second half but another converted Widnes try opened up an eighteen point gap between the sides. Roy Haggerty sold a huge dummy to register Saints' first try of the game but Widnes immediately hit back with another try to put them 26-10 ahead. Barry Ledger's try reduced the gap but further tries from McKenzie and Tait emphasised the gulf between the two sides on the day. Widnes had scored seven tries to Saints' two and had repeatedly opened up a porous defence. In the circumstances it was remarkable that Offiah did not get onto the scoresheet.

SAINTS 14 – WIDNES 38

Man of the match: David Hulme

Programme cover from the 1988 Premiership final at Old Trafford.

FINAL FACT

Alan Tait won a winner's medal despite never having started a game of Rugby League. The Scottish union international had signed for Widnes in April and had played as a substitute in each of their three Premiership Trophy matches.

1992 PREMIERSHIP FINAL

SUNDAY 17 MAY at OLD TRAFFORD, MANCHESTER

SAINTS v WIGAN

SPONSOR: STONES BITTER

SAINTS	WIGAN
Phil VEIVERS	Steve HAMPSON
Alan HUNTE	Joe LYDON
Gary CONNOLLY	Dean BELL (Capt)
Paul LOUGHLIN *Try and 2 Goals*	Gene MILES *Try*
Anthony SULLIVAN 2 *Tries*	Martin OFFIAH 2 *Tries*
Tea ROPATI	Frano BOTICA *10 Goals*
Paul BISHOP	Shaun EDWARDS
Jonathan NEIL	Neil COWIE
Bernard DWYER	Martin DERMOTT
Kevin WARD	Andy PLATT *Try*
Sonny NICKLE	Denis BETTS *2 Tries*
George MANN	Billy McGINTY
Shane COOPER (Capt)	Phil CLARKE
Substitutes	Substitutes
Jonathan GRIFFITHS	David MYERS *Try*
Paul GROVES	Sam PANAPA
Coach: Mike McClennan	Coach: John Monie

Referee: John Holdsworth (Kippax)

Attendance: 33,157

Saints had finished the league season in second position, eight points behind champions Wigan. This guaranteed them home ties in the lead up to the final. They crushed Halifax (7th) 52-6 in the quarter final and comfortably defeated Castleford (3rd) 30-14 in the semi-final. Meanwhile Wigan had racked up 116 points in hammering Widnes and Leeds. Offiah scored ten tries in their semi-final!

Such was the strength of Wigan's squad that thirteen of their players were selected for the Great Britain's 1992 Australasian tour. Miles, Botica, Bell and Panapa added further quality to the team. Saints had four players selected. Gary Connolly, Paul Loughlin and Sonny Nickle were in the original squad and Alan Hunte was called up to replace the injured Jonathan Davies.

The Stretford End was being prepared for demolition and so the ground capacity was reduced to 33,157. A full house watched Saints wilt under a second half Wigan onslaught.

A tight opening eighteen minutes saw Paul Loughlin and Botica exchange penalties before Saints captain Shane Cooper was sent to the sin bin for kicking out. Wigan swiftly capitalised on their numerical advantage and Platt dummied his way over for a converted try and Botica also kicked a penalty. However, Saints rallied and tries from Anthony Sullivan and Loughlin, together with a Loughlin goal, deservedly put Saints 12-10 up at the break.

Sadly for Saints supporters, that was as good as it got. Ten minutes after the interval Miles sent Offiah racing away to put Wigan back in front. Wigan then proceeded to demolish Saints with a procession of tries, all converted by the immaculate Botica. In just twenty five minutes Wigan turned a 10-12 deficit into a 48-12 lead. Saints appeared powerless to resist and conceded two tries to Betts, one each to Miles and Myers and a second to Offiah. Sullivan's last minute try was no consolation for what had been a truly disastrous second half showing from Saints and a magnificent one from their bitter rivals.

SAINTS 16 – WIGAN 48

Man of the match: Andy Platt

FINAL FACT

Wigan's score of 48 points was the highest of any side in a major final in the game's then 97 year old history. It remains the highest number of points conceded by Saints in any of the finals that they have contested.

1993 PREMIERSHIP FINAL

SUNDAY 16 MAY at OLD TRAFFORD, MANCHESTER

SAINTS v WIGAN

SPONSOR: STONES BITTER

SAINTS	WIGAN
David LYON	Paul ATCHESON
Mike RILEY	Jason ROBINSON
Gary CONNOLLY *Try*	Sam PANAPA
Paul LOUGHLIN *Try*	Andrew FARRAR
Alan HUNTE	Martin OFFIAH
Tea ROPATI	Frano BOTICA
Gus O'DONNELL 2 *DG*	Sean EDWARDS (Capt)
Jonathan NEILL	Neil COWIE
Bernard DWYER	Martin DERMOTT
George MANN	Kelvin SKERRETT
Chris JOYNT	Mick CASSIDY
Sonny NICKLE	Andrew FARRELL
Shane COOPER (Capt)	Phil CLARKE
Substitutes	Substitutes
Jonathan GRIFFITHS	Mike FORSHAW *Try*
Phil VEIVERS	Ian GILDART
Coach: Mike McClennan	Coach: John Monie

Referee: John Holdsworth (Kippax)

Attendance: 36,598

Saints and Wigan were both eleven points clear of third placed Bradford Northern in the 1992/93 league table. However, Wigan took the championship title on points difference. The Central Park team had also won the Challenge Cup, Regal Trophy and Lancashire Cup and were seeking a history making Grand Slam of all five major trophies.

Saints defeated seventh placed Halifax 34-25 in first round of the top eight play-offs before seeing off Leeds 15-2 in the semi-final.

The match was the final part of a triple header, having been preceded by the Academy final between Hull and Warrington and the Divisional final between Featherstone Rovers and Workington Town.

The match was an attritional affair, with defences on top throughout. A scoreless first half looked likely until Saints were the beneficiaries of a vital piece of good fortune. Shane Cooper dabbed a kick to the Wigan line and when it deflected off a defender Gary Connolly was on hand to touch down to break the deadlock. Paul Loughlin missed his conversion attempt but the Saints held a 4-0 lead at the interval.

Saints' defence held firm until the hour mark when after a period of sustained pressure Botica's pass put substitute Forshaw in at the corner. Botica was arguably the most reliable goal kicker the game has ever seen but his conversion attempt hit the post and bounced away and so the sides were level with twenty minutes remaining. Gus O'Donnell had been unable to secure a first team place at star studded Wigan and so had signed for Saints. He showed great presence of mind to slot over drop goals in the 63rd and 68th minutes to edge Saints into a 6-4 lead over his old club.

Just five minutes remained when fine cross field passing created enough space for Paul Loughlin to score in the left-hand corner. However, he was unable to convert his try and Saints had to defend a six point lead for the final minutes. They did so and so won the Premiership Trophy for the fourth and final time.

Saints' players were understandably delighted to end the season on a high and ensured that Kevin Ward, who had suffered a career ending injury in the Good Friday draw with Wigan, was fully included in the post-match celebrations.

SAINTS 10 – WIGAN 4

Man of the match: Chris Joynt

FINAL FACT

Wigan had won the previous nineteen finals in which they had appeared. Their last defeat in a final had been when Saints had beaten them in the 1984 Lancashire Cup Final.

Captain Shane Cooper holds the Premiership Trophy aloft after Saints' unexpected victory over Wigan at Old Trafford in the 1993 final. Kiwi Shane played 271 times for Saints between 1987 and 1995, scoring 76 tries.
(© Copyright rlphotos.com)

Programme cover from the 1992 Premiership Final.

1996 PREMIERSHIP FINAL

SUNDAY 8 SEPTEMBER at OLD TRAFFORD, MANCHESTER

SAINTS v WIGAN

SPONSOR: STONES

SAINTS	WIGAN
Steve PRESCOTT	Kris RADLINSKI
Joey HAYES	Danny ELLISON *3 Tries*
Alan HUNTE	Gary CONNOLLY *Try*
Paul NEWLOVE *Try*	Va'aiga TUIGAMALA
Anthony SULLIVAN	Jason ROBINSON *Try*
Tommy MARTYN *Try*	Henry PAUL *Try*
Bobbie Goulding (Capt) *3 Goals*	Shaun EDWARDS *Try*
Apollo PERELINI	Kelvin SKERRETT
Keiron CUNNINGHAM	Martin HALL
Adam FOGERTY	Terry O'CONNOR
Derek McVEY	Simon HAUGHTON *Try*
Chris MORLEY	Mick CASSIDY
Karle HAMMOND	Andrew FARRELL (Capt) *4 Goals*
Substitutes	Substitutes
Ian PICKAVANCE	Neil COWIE
Danny ARNOLD	Steve BARROW
Simon BOOTH	Andrew JOHNSON
Andy HAIGH	Craig MURDOCH Try
Coach: Shaun McRae	Coach: Graeme West

Referee: David Campbell

Attendance: 35,013

1996 was the first season of the Super League era. Saints had enjoyed a tremendous season, defeating Bradford Bulls in an epic Challenge Cup final and winning the inaugural Stones Super League Championship, ending Wigan's record seven year reign as league champions.

It had been decided to retain the Premiership competition but it was modified so that only the top four teams took part. Saints beat London Broncos 25-14 in one semi-final and Wigan defeated Bradford Bulls 42-36 in the other.

Wigan started well and ex-Saint Connolly scored the game's opening try in the tenth minute after he spotted a gap at a play-the-ball and dashed forty metres to the line. Saints quickly responded with a Paul Newlove try, converted by Bobbie Goulding. Wigan regained the lead in the 22nd minute when Farrell put Edwards in for a try which he then converted. Another Farrell pass put Ellison in for his first try to increase Saints' deficit to eight points. Goulding kicked a penalty but Wigan led 18-8 at half time thanks to a spectacular try from Ellison.

Saints started the second half strongly and after 48 minutes Tommy Martyn scored a good try, converted by Goulding, which raised the hopes of Saints' supporters. However, Wigan dominated the remainder of the game and scored five unanswered tries, three of which Farrell converted. Tries from Houghton, Paul and Robinson put Wigan into an unassailable 34-14 lead after 67 minutes and further late scores from Murdoch and Ellison turned a disappointing defeat into a real hammering. To add injury to insult Paul Newlove went off late in the game with a hamstring injury which ruled him out of Great Britain's South Pacific tour.

SAINTS 14 - WIGAN 44

Man of the match: Andrew Farrell

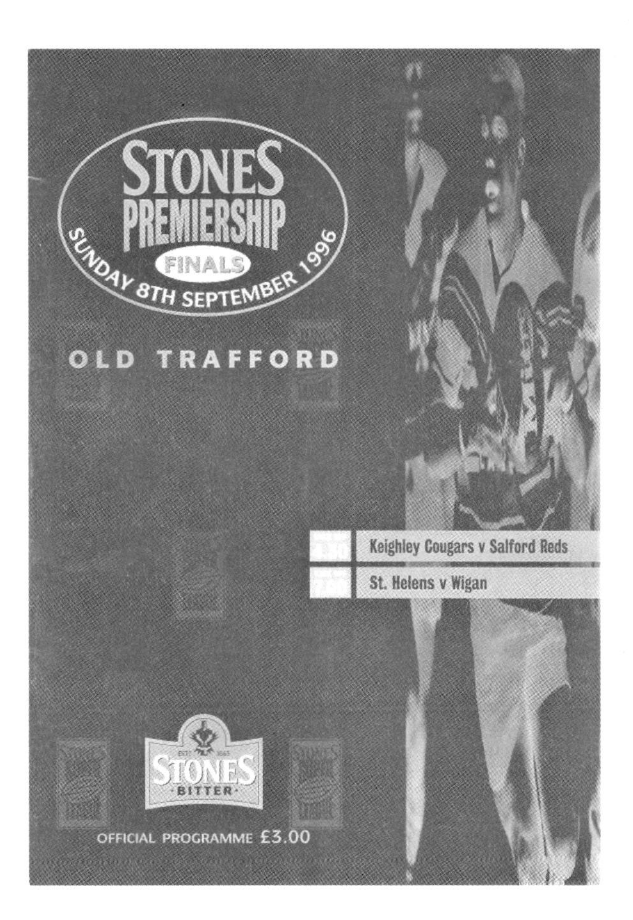

Programme cover of the 1996 Premiership final.

FINAL FACT

This was the last game that Saints' great rivals played as simply 'Wigan.' They were rebranded as Wigan Warriors in readiness for the 1997 season.

1997 PREMIERSHIP FINAL

SUNDAY 28 SEPTEMBER at OLD TRAFFORD, MANCHESTER

SAINTS v WIGAN WARRIORS

SPONSOR: STONES

SAINTS	**WIGAN WARRIORS**
Danny ARNOLD	Jason ROBINSON *Try*
Anthony STEWART	Andy JOHNSON *Try*
Alan HUNTE	Kris RADLINSKI *Try*
Paul NEWLOVE *Try*	Gary CONNOLLY
Anthony SULLIVAN	Danny ELLISON
Karle HAMMOND *Try*	Henry PAUL
Sean LONG 2 Goals	Tony SMITH
Andy LEATHAM	Neil COWIE
Keiron CUNNINGHAM	John CLARKE
Julian O'NEILL	Lee HANSEN
Apollo PERELINI	Simon HAUGHTON *Try*
Derek McVEY *Try*	Mick CASSIDY
Chris JOYNT (Capt)	Andrew FARRELL (Capt) *Try,6 Goals*
Substitutes	Substitutes
Ian PICKAVANCE	Nigel WRIGHT DG
Chris MORLEY	Terry O'CONNOR
Simon BOOTH	Stephen HOLGATE
Paul ANDERSON *Try*	Gael TELLEC
Coach: Shaun McRae	Coach: Eric Hughes

Referee: Stuart Cummings

Attendance: 33,389

The previous season had seen just the top four teams compete for the end of season Premiership trophy. However, the 1997 competition included all twelve Super League sides. Saints, who had finished third, were exempt from the preliminary round and met sixth placed Salford Reds in the quarter final and won by 26 points to 12. Tenth placed Castleford Tigers led 18-2 at Knowsley Road in the semi-final but Saints scored five unanswered tries in the final thirty minutes to win 32-18.

Wigan were playing in their seventh consecutive Premiership final and had won all but one of the previous six. However, they had had a disappointing season and only finished fourth in the league table.

If Saints supporters thought Wigan were no longer automatic favourites to win any final they were soon reminded of the Warriors' ability. In the fourth minute Farrell's well-judged kick was caught by Johnson, who touched down for the game's opening try. Farrell missed the conversion but soon afterwards landed a penalty to put the Warriors 6-0 ahead. Derek McVey's try reduced the arrears but another Farrell penalty was followed by a scruffy Robinson try and the conversion put Wigan 14-4 up with half an hour played. In the 34th minute Paul Newlove showed his pace and power to score following a forty metre run. Saints therefore trailed 8-14 at the interval.

Sean Long kicked his first goal just two minutes into the second half to reduce the gap but Wigan scored nineteen points in the next twenty minutes to crush Saints' hopes. Radlinski, Farrell and Haughton scored tries and Farrell kicked three more goals, with Wright adding a drop goal. Saints rallied in the final few minutes and tries from Paul Anderson and Karle Hammond, together with a conversion by Long, gave the score a slightly more respectable appearance. However, as in the previous Premiership final, Saints had been well beaten by their oldest rivals and Wigan captain Farrell was presented with both the trophy and the man of the match award.

SAINTS 20 - WIGAN WARRIORS 33

Programme cover of the last ever Premiership final.

FINAL FACT

This was the last ever Premiership final. It was decided to introduce an Australian style play-off, culminating in a Grand Final, to determine the 1998 Super League champions and after twenty-three seasons the Premiership competition ceased to exist.

JOHN PLAYER SPECIAL/REGAL TROPHY FINALS

This unseeded knock-out competition was organised on similar lines to the Challenge Cup and was always played in the first half of the season, with the final usually taking place in January. It was introduced in 1971/72 and lasted until 1995/96. The introduction of Super League and summer rugby meant that it had no place in the new season's calendar.

The sponsor throughout its 25 seasons was Imperial Tobacco. However the competition's title varied depending on which brand of cigarettes the sponsor wished to promote. At various times it was called the John Player No. 6 Trophy, The John Player Special Trophy and the Regal Trophy.

Saints only reached the final twice. They defeated Leeds 15-14 at Central Park, Wigan in the 1987/88 final, watched by 16,669 and lost to Wigan 16-25 in the last ever final in 1995/96 at the McAlpine Stadium in Huddersfield, when the attendance was 17,590.

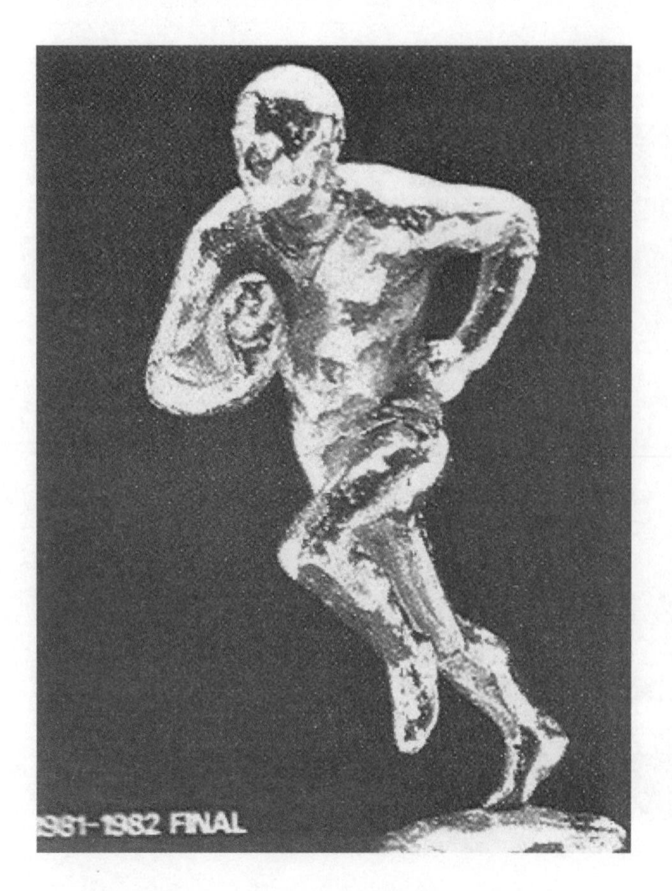

This photograph of the John Player Trophy appeared in the 1981/82 final programme

The competition was re-branded as the Regal Trophy from 1989/90 until 1995/96

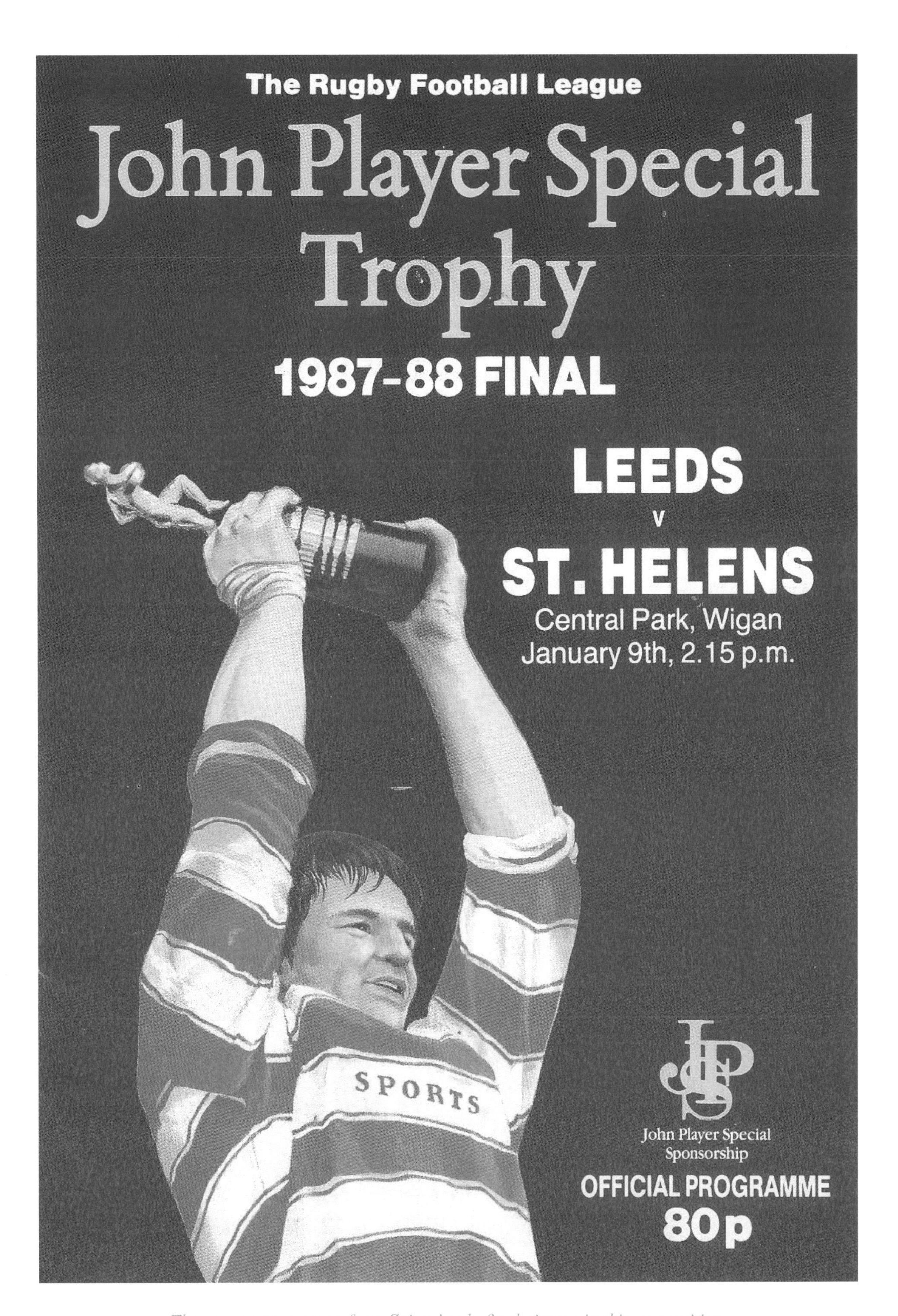

The programme cover from Saints' only final victory in this competition.

1988 JOHN PLAYER SPECIAL TROPHY FINAL

SATURDAY 9 JANUARY 1988 at CENTRAL PARK, WIGAN

SAINTS v LEEDS SPONSOR: IMPERIAL TOBACCO

SAINTS	LEEDS
Phil VEIVERS	Marty GURR
David TANNER	Steve MORRIS
Paul LOUGHLIN 2 *Tries and 3 Goals*	Garry SCHOFIELD
Mark ELIA	Peter JACKSON *Try*
Les QUIRK	John BASNETT
Shane COOPER (Capt)	David CREASSER *Try and 3 Goals*
Neil HOLDING *DG*	Ray ASHTON
Tony BURKE	Peter TUNKS (Capt)
Paul GROVES	Colin MASKILL
Peter SOUTO	Kevin RAYNE
Paul FORBER	Roy POWELL
Roy HAGGERTY	Paul MEDLEY
Andy PLATT	David HERON
Substitutes	Substitutes
David LARGE	Carl GIBSON
Stuart EVANS	John FAIRBANK
Coach: Alex Murphy	Coach: Maurice Bamford

Referee: Fred Lindop (Wakefield) Attendance: 16,669

Saints had fallen at the semi-final hurdle five times since the inception of the JPS trophy in 1971/72 but managed to reach the final for the first time in 1987/88. They were assisted by receiving home draws in each of the first three rounds. They edged Widnes out by 12 points to 10 in the first round and easily defeated Mansfield Marksmen 40-0 in round two. Hull put up a good fight in the quarter final but Saints prevailed by 20 points to 16. The semi-final against Oldham was played at Wigan and Saints' 18-8 victory earned them a place in the final.

Both teams put on a great show which lit up a grey January afternoon. Leeds stand-off Creasser opened the scoring after thirteen minutes when Powell's pass put him in the clear and he then kicked the conversion to put Leeds 6-0 ahead. Paul Loughlin replied with a penalty and in the 25th minute he put Saints in front when referee Lindop ignored Leeds appeals for a double movement and awarded his try between the posts, which he easily converted. Creasser squared the scores with a successful penalty and then put the Yorkshire side ahead when he scored a try after Peter Souto lost the ball in a tackle. His conversion put Leeds 14-8 ahead but a Neil Holding drop goal on the stroke of half time reduced the deficit to five points.

Two minutes into the second half man of the match Loughlin scored what proved to be the game's crucial try. Paul Forber fed the centre and he showed strength and speed to cut inside Basnett and Gurr to score underneath the posts. His conversion edged Saints 15-14 ahead. As the pitch became increasingly heavy Leeds struggled to break down a resolute Saints defence. Schofield almost drew Leeds level with a drop goal attempt which hit the post but Saints held on to lift the trophy and secure the £16,000 prize money.

SAINTS 15 - LEEDS 14

Man of the match: Paul Loughlin

The Saints squad for the JPS final.
Back Row (Left to Right): Haggerty, Evans, Burke, Forber, Loughlin, Elia, Fieldhouse, Quirk, Cooper
Middle Row (Left to Right): Large, McCormack, Arkwright, Platt, Groves, Tanner, Veivers
Front row (Left to Right): Holding, Liptrot, Ledger, Bailey
Also in the picture are John Meadows (kit man), Alex Murphy (coach) and
Dave Chisnall (assistant coach).

FINAL FACT

This was the only time Saints won this trophy. In fact they only competed in two of the competition's 25 finals.

1996 REGAL TROPHY FINAL

SATURDAY 13 JANUARY at McALPINE STADIUM, HUDDERSFIELD

SAINTS V WIGAN

SPONSOR: IMPERIAL TOBACCO

SAINTS	WIGAN
Steve PRESCOTT	Gary CONNOLLY
Joey HAYES *Try*	Jason ROBINSON
Scott GIBBS	Va'aiga TUIGAMALA *Try*
Paul NEWLOVE *Try*	Kris RADLINSKI *Try*
Anthony SULLIVAN	Martin OFFIAH
Karle HAMMOND	Henry PAUL 2 *Tries and 4 Goals*
Bobbie GOULDING (Capt) 2 *Goals*	Shaun EDWARDS (Capt) *DG*
Apollo PERELINI	Neil COWIE
Keiron CUNNINGHAM *Try*	Martin HALL
Ian PICKAVANCE	Terry O'CONNOR
Chris JOYNT	Scott QUINNELL
Simon BOOTH	Mick CASSIDY
Dean BUSBY	Simon HAUGHTON
Substitutes	Substitutes
Andy NORTHEY	Rob SMYTH
Vila MATAUTIA	Martin DERMOTT
Coach: Eric Hughes	Coach: Graeme West

Referee: Russell Smith

Attendance: 17,590

Saints, along with the other teams from the first and second divisions, entered the competition at the second round stage and won comfortably at Keighley Cougars by 42 points to 14. They travelled to the Boulevard to meet Hull in the next round and registered a 38-26 victory. Halifax visited Knowsley Round in the quarter final and were dispatched by 46 points to 18. Saints then defeated Warrington at Knowsley Road by the incredible score of 80-0 to reach the final.

Remarkably, Saints had only participated in one of the previous twenty-four finals and went into the match as underdogs as their opponents were Wigan, who were appearing in their fourth consecutive final.

The huge Wigan centre Tuigamala powered over for the game's opening try after a quarter of an hour's play and Paul converted. However, Saints hit back strongly and Joey Hayes finished off an excellent move to score a fine try. Paul Newlove then put Saints in the lead with a try but unfortunately Bobbie Goulding was unable to convert either try. Nonetheless Saints led 8-6 at the interval.

However, six minutes into the second half Wigan regained the lead with a soft try. Scott Gibbs lost the ball on his own line and Radlinski pounced to score and Paul converted. Six minutes later Paul put Wigan 18-8 ahead when he danced past three defenders to score a try which he converted. Goulding landed a penalty to make it 10-18 but an Edwards drop goal edged Wigan nine points clear. In the 70th minute man of the match Keiron Cunningham stretched an arm out in a tackle near the Wigan line to score despite being surrounded by a posse of Wigan defenders and Goulding's conversion made to score 16-19 to set up a rousing finale. However, Saints could not strike the killer blow and with the final hooter approaching Gibbs was dismissed for illegal use of his elbow in fending off a Wigan tackler. Saints' frustration was complete when Paul scored his second try in the final minute and his conversion was the final act of the match.

The start of the new Super League was just over two months away and although Saints supporters were disappointed to lose to their old rivals, nonetheless there was a growing belief that the switch to summer rugby would be beneficial to Saints' style of play and that the long era of Wigan dominance could be coming to an end.

SAINTS 16 - WIGAN 25

Man of the match: Keiron Cunningham

FINAL FACT

This was the last final of what is now known as the 'Pre-Super League era.' The opening round of Super League fixtures were played at the end of March 1996 and the Regal Trophy was not to be a part of the brave new world of summer rugby.

LANCASHIRE CUP FINALS

This unseeded knock-out competition ran from 1905/06 until 1992/93. It was competed for by clubs located in the old county of Lancashire. As the game expanded teams from Cumberland also entered and in the 1980s teams such as Fulham, who were situated two hundred or so miles south of Lancashire, also participated. The competition was completed in the early part of the season, with the final usually taking place in October or November.

- Saints played in 19 finals, winning eleven and losing eight. Their victory in 1967 came in a replay.
- Saints' highest score was 30 v Oldham (1968)
- Opponents' highest score was 22 v Leigh (1952)
- Saints' biggest margin of victory was 28 v Oldham (1968)
- Saints' biggest margin of defeat was 17 v Leigh (1952)
- The highest attendance at any Lancashire Cup Final in which Saints have played was 42,793 v Wigan (1953)
- The lowest attendance at any Lancashire Cup Final in which Saints have played was 6,462 v Warrington (1982)
- 11 of the finals were played at Central Park, Wigan. Six, including one replay, were played at Station Road, Swinton, two at Wilderspool, Warrington and the last final in 1992 was played at Knowsley Road
- None of grounds at which Saints played finals are still in use
- Saints played in seven consecutive finals between 1958 and 1964. They lost the first two and then won five on the trot

Programme covers from the 1952 and 1953 Lancashire Cup finals

1926 LANCASHIRE CUP FINAL

SATURDAY 20 NOVEMBER at WILDERSPOOL, WARRINGTON

SAINTS v ST HELENS RECS

SAINTS	ST HELENS RECS
Charlie CROOKS	Tommy DINGSDALE
George COTTON	Jack WILSON
Alf FRODSHAM	Albert BAILEY
George LEWIS 2 *Goals*	Jim PYKE *Goal*
Alf ELLABY *Try*	Jack WALLACE
Leslie FAIRCLOUGH *Try*	Johnny GREENALL (Capt)
Walter GROVES	Jack HALSALL
Bob ATKIN	Tommy HIGGINS
Albert SIMM	Oliver DOLAN
Bill CLAREY	George HIGHCOCK
Lou HOUGHTON	Tommy SMITH
Fred ROFFEY (Capt)	Albert FILDES
Ernie SHAW	Bill MULVANNEY

Referee: Mr H. Horsfall (Batley) Attendance: 19,439

Saints won their first ever major trophy in 1926 when they beat local rivals St Helens Recs in the Lancashire Cup final in what was to prove to be the only all-St Helens cup final in history.

Saints hammered amateur side Pemberton Rovers 51-8 in the first round and then defeated Swinton 29-18 in round two. Saints were drawn away to Widnes in the semi-final and managed a 3-3 draw before coasting to a 17-0 victory in the replay at Knowsley Road to reach the final for the very first time. Recs were no strangers to the final however, having won the trophy in 1923 and been runners-up in 1924. They were therefore widely regarded as favourites.

Driving rain greeted the players as they stepped onto the pitch in front of a passionate crowd. George Lewis kicked a penalty goal after just a minute's play to calm Saints supporters' nerves. After fifteen minutes Leslie Fairclough showed great skill to pick up Alf Frodsham's grubber kick and swerve past Fildes to score under the posts. Lewis converted to put Saints 7-0 ahead. Star winger Alf Ellaby then showed his quality when he chipped over Wilson and dribbled the ball to the line before scoring in the corner. Although Pyke landed a penalty goal for Recs just before half time, Saints went in at the interval with a healthy eight point advantage.

Conditions deteriorated in the second half as the pitch turned into a sea of mud and it became increasingly difficult to distinguish the players as their kit became covered in mud. The defence of both teams was strong and try as they might neither side could add to their score. When Mr Horsfall blew the final whistle Saints supporters jumped over the barriers to congratulate the players on a famous victory.

Saints returned in triumph to the Town Hall before retiring to the club's headquarters, the White Lion hotel, to continue their celebrations.

Saints would have to wait until 1953 before they lifted the Lancashire Cup trophy again. By then Recs had resigned from the league, as Pilkingtons withdrew their financial support for the club after the Second World War.

SAINTS 10 - ST HELENS RECS 2

FINAL FACT

St Helens Recs appeared in five Lancashire Cup finals between the wars and lifted the trophy on two occasions. In contrast Saints only appeared in two finals between 1905 and 1951.

1932 LANCASHIRE CUP FINAL

SATURDAY 19 NOVEMBER at CENTRAL PARK, WIGAN

SAINTS v WARRINGTON

SAINTS	WARRINGTON
Bob JONES	Billy HOLDING 2 *Goals*
Roy HARDGRAVE	Thomas THOMPSON *Try*
George LEWIS (Capt) 3 *Goals*	Billy DINGSDALE
Teddy BUTLER	Bill SHANKLAND (Capt)
Alf ELLABY	Steve RAY
Jack GARVEY	Jack OSTER
Harry FRODSHAM	Dai DAVIES *Try*
Bob ATKIN	Jack MILLER
Dave COTTON	Nat BENTHAM
Ben HALFPENNY	Sammy HARDMAN
Albert FILDES *Try*	Bill JONES
Jack ARKWRIGHT	Candy EVANS
Walter GROVES	Charlie SEELING

Referee: Mr Brown

Attendance: 28,500

Having won the Championship trophy for the first time in 1932, Saints supporters hoped for more silverware in the 1932/33 season. Saints were given a tough away draw at Widnes in the first round but secured a 10-5 victory, thanks to two tries from Roy Hardgrave. Saints comfortably beat Broughton Rangers 22-4 in round two before drawing 2-2 in a very tight semi-final at Salford. The replay at Knowsley Road was a much more open affair and Saints triumphed by 17 points to 10 to secure a place in the Lancashire Cup final for only the second time in their history.

There was great interest in the match and the attendance set a new Lancashire Cup final record. Regular centres Tom Winnard and Bill Mercer were both injured and their presence was missed by Saints.

Saints opened the scoring with a George Lewis penalty but, somewhat against the run of play, Warrington took the lead with a fine try by Davies, converted by Holding. However, Saints regained the lead when Dave Cotton and Jack Arkwright combined well to put Albert Fildes into space and he raced twenty-five yards to the try line. Lewis converted to put Saints 7-5 ahead at the interval.

However, Holding levelled things up with a successful penalty before Thompson scored what proved to be a match winning try for Warrington. Oster's pass put Dingsdale into space and he drew Alf Ellaby before sending Thompson over with a well-timed pass. The conversion was missed and another Lewis penalty reduced the gap to a single point. Saints pressed hard but both Butler and Lewis failed to convert overlaps into tries and Warrington held out for the victory.

Saints returned home to be entertained in the mayor's parlour but in truth there was little to celebrate after such a close defeat.

SAINTS 9 - WARRINGTON 10

FINAL FACT

This match was to be Saints' last final appearance before the outbreak of World War II in 1939. In fact it would be 1952 before Saints reached another final.

1952 LANCASHIRE CUP FINAL

SATURDAY 29 NOVEMBER at STATION ROAD, SWINTON

SAINTS v LEIGH

SAINTS	LEIGH
Jim LOWE	Jim LEDGARD (Capt) *5 Goals*
Steve LLEWELLYN	Brian CHADWICK *Try*
Duggie GREENALL (Capt)	Trevor ALLAN *Try*
Don GULLICK *Try*	Ted KERWICK
Stan McCORMICK	Frank KITCHEN 2 *Tries*
Jimmy HONEY	Ken BAXTER
George LANGFIELD *Goal*	Tommy BRADSHAW
Alan PRESCOTT	Harry EDDEN
Reg BLAKEMORE	Joe EGAN
Bill WHITTAKER	Stan OWEN
George PARSONS	Charlie PAWSEY
Bill BRETHERTON	Rex MOSSOP
Ray CALE	Peter FOSTER
Coach: Jim Sullivan	Player Coach: Joe Egan

Referee: Mr A Hill   Attendance: 34,785

The first round was played over two legs. Saints' won narrowly 24-21 at Barrow and then comfortably won 23-5 at Knowsley Road for a 47-26 aggregate victory. Rochdale Hornets visited Saints in round two and were easily defeated by 31 points to 7. Saints travelled to Wilderspool in the semi-final and triumphed over Warrington by 17 points to 10.

Leigh were competing in their seventh Lancashire Cup final but had never managed to win the trophy before and started as underdogs. With coach Jim Sullivan at the helm Saints had made a strong start to the season and the many Saints supporters in the large crowd were confident that it would be seventh time unlucky for Leigh. Few, if any, would have predicted that Leigh would not merely win but completely outplay Saints.

Ledgard opened the scoring with a penalty goal after a quarter of an hour but almost immediately Saints were level when George Langfield slotted over a penalty. Saints were looking surprisingly nervous and normally reliable players were fumbling simple passes. Jimmy Honey lost possession in the 25th minute and winger Kitchen took full advantage to score. Saints handling woes continued and just minutes later another spilled ball was quickly worked to Kitchen, who again made no mistake. Leigh's third try was the best of the match. Kerwick made a superb break and his long pass found winger Chadwick who touched down. Ledgard's conversion put Leigh 13-2 up and his subsequent penalty put Leigh further ahead as half time approached.

In the second half Leigh continued with the simple but successful tactic of getting the ball to Ledgard, whose long kicks downfield meant Saints spent long periods pinned down in their own 25 yard area. Leigh were in full control and another penalty goal gave them an impregnable fifteen point lead. Towards the end Don Gullick scored Saints only try after a good break from Langfield. However, Leigh had the final word when Allan scored their fourth try in the last minute. Mr Hill blew his whistle for the last time immediately after Ledgard's conversion. At the seventh time of asking the Lancashire Cup was at last on its way to Leigh, whilst Saints supporters would have to wait a little longer to celebrate winning their first trophy since 1932.

SAINTS 5 - LEIGH 22

FINAL FACT

This was the first Lancashire Cup final since the war which did not feature Wigan as one of the finalists. They lost to Widnes in the 1945 final and then won the next six in a row. However, Leigh had beaten them 19-8 in the second round in 1952.

1953 LANCASHIRE CUP FINAL

SATURDAY 24 OCTOBER at STATION ROAD, SWINTON

SAINTS v WIGAN

SAINTS	WIGAN
Glyn MOSES *Try*	Jack CUNLIFFE
Steve LLEWELLYN	Brian NORDGREN
Duggie GREENALL (Capt)	Jack BROOME
Don GULLICK	Ernie ASHCROFT
Stan McCORMICK	Ronnie HURST
Peter METCALFE *5 Goals*	Jack FLEMING *Try*
Jimmy HONEY *Try*	Johnny ALTY
Alan PRESCOTT	Ken GEE (Capt) *Goal*
Reg BLAKEMORE	Ronnie MATHER
George PARR	Nat SILCOCK
George PARSONS	Frank COLLIER
Billy BRETHERTON	Tommy HORROCKS
Vince KARALIUS	Harry STREET *Try*
Coach: Jim Sullivan	Coach: Ted Ward

Referee: Mr M Coates (Pudsey) Attendance: 42,793

The first round of the competition was played over two legs. Saints lost 13-14 at Barrow in the first leg but won the second leg 21-17 to record a narrow 34-31 aggregate victory. Saints easily defeated Swinton 38-9 at Knowsley Road in the second round and their reward was a home semi-final against Warrington, which they won 17-10 to reach the final for the second successive year. Their opponents in the final were fierce rivals Wigan and a massive crowd of over 42,000 crammed into Station Road to watch the clash.

Gee had already missed two penalty attempts for Wigan before Peter Metcalfe put Saints in the lead with a successful kick. Wigan had the majority of the best attacking opportunities and Street forced his way over for the game's opening try. Collier tried his luck with the conversion but missed. Fleming and Nordgren then combined well for Wigan's second try, which Gee converted to put Wigan 8-2 ahead. However, Metcalfe kicked another penalty to make it Saints 4 Wigan 8 at the interval.

Saints continued to concede penalties in the early part of the second half but Gee missed two kicks and Collier one so the score remained unchanged until Metcalfe showed how it should be done by kicking his third penalty goal. After being second best for most of the game Saints took the lead with a try from Jimmy Honey which Metcalfe converted. Saints were buoyed up and when Glyn Moses collected Steve Llewellyn's cross kick to score Saints' second try they took control of the game. Metcalfe's trusty boot added the conversion to put Saints 16-8 ahead and the cup was theirs for only the second time ever. Both sides had scored a brace of tries but Peter Metcalfe had kicked five goals whilst Gee and Collier had spurned numerous opportunities and only landed one between them.

SAINTS 16 - WIGAN 8

FINAL FACT

The attendance of 42,793 was highest of any county final in history. The highest ever Yorkshire Cup final attendance was 36,000, whilst the next highest Lancashire Cup final attendance was 42,541.

1956 LANCASHIRE CUP FINAL

SATURDAY 20 OCTOBER at CENTRAL PARK, WIGAN

SAINTS v OLDHAM

SAINTS	OLDHAM
Glyn MOSES	Bernard GANLEY 2 *Goals*
Steve LLEWELLYN	Dick CRACKNELL
Duggie GREENALL	Dennis AYRES
Bill FINNAN	Alan DAVIES
Frank CARLTON *Try*	John ETTY *Try*
Austin RHODES	Frank STIRRUP (Capt)
John 'Todder' DICKINSON	Frank PITCHFORD
Alan PRESCOTT (Capt)	Ken JACKSON
Len McINTYRE	Jack KEITH
Nat SILCOCK	Don VINES
George PARSONS	Sid LITTLE
John GASKELL	Charlie WINSLADE
Vince KARALIUS	Derek TURNER *Try*
Coach: Jim Sullivan	Coach: Griff Jenkins

Referee: Mr M Coates (Pudsey) Attendance: 39,544

Saints played Swinton at home in the first round and won comfortably, 27-7. Liverpool City visited Knowsley Road in round two and were swept aside 34-3. Warrington provided stiffer opposition at Wilderspool in the semi-final but Saints prevailed 17-9.

Although Oldham had not won a trophy for twenty years they had assembled a strong side and were the only Lancashire team to have beaten Saints in the league prior to the final. The programme notes complained that the emphasis on winning led to 'a team gaining a lead and sticking to it by playing negative football.' Unfortunately this was the case in the final and the spectacle was a great disappointment to the huge crowd who crammed into Central Park. Possession was dominated by the forwards and the talented backs got very few opportunities to show their skill and speed.

Ganley kicked a penalty to put Oldham ahead in the sixth minute. After a quarter of an hour Turner intercepted a pass and flung the ball out to winger Etty who touched down. Saints were struggling to find any cohesion and it came as a great surprise when Frank Carlton was given a rare chance by Len

McIntyre. He accelerated past Cracknell and raced around Ganley. Pitchford covered across and managed to knock Carlton to the ground but the Saints winger regained his feet and staggered over for an excellent try. However, the conversion was missed and another Ganley penalty put Oldham 7-3 up at the interval.

The second half was described by one reporter as 'grim, relentless and unbearably drab.' The play resembled trench warfare as the two packs battered into each other without making any significant progress whilst the backs looked on as mere spectators. However, this state of affairs suited Oldham, who never looked like losing their lead. With just a minute remaining Turner sealed victory with a try and Oldham's long wait for a trophy was over.

SAINTS 3 - OLDHAM 10

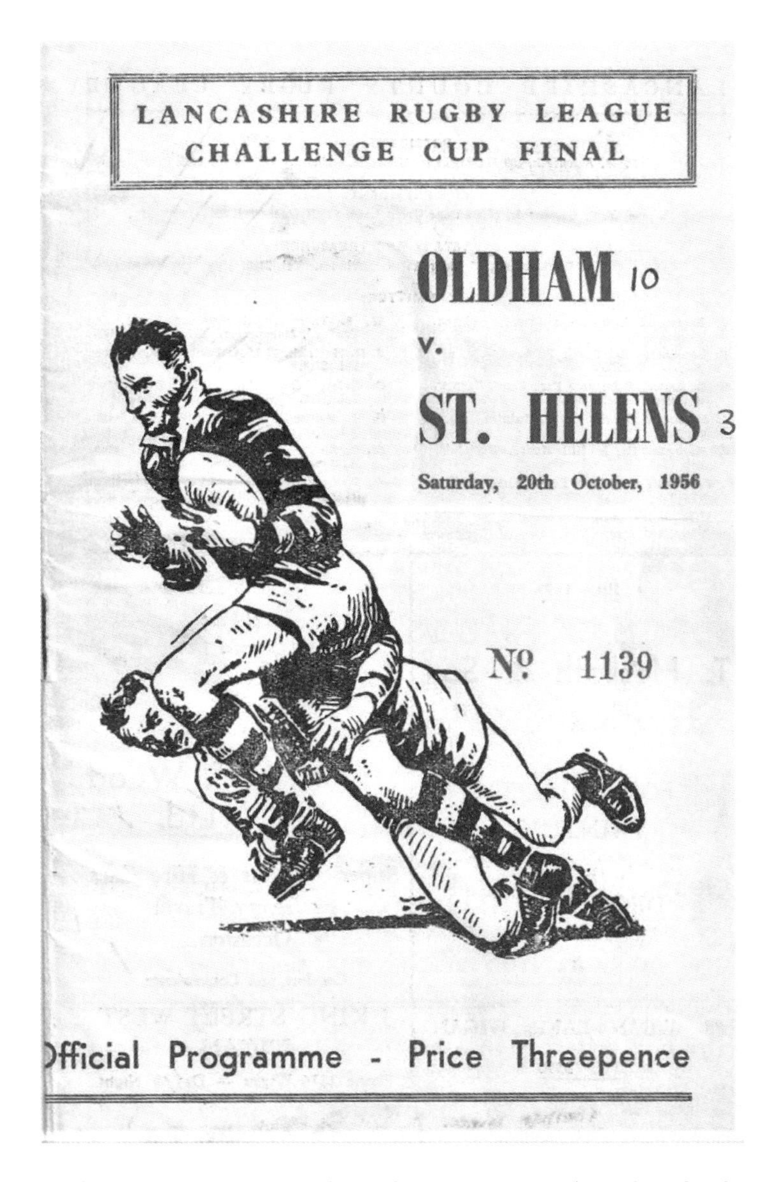

The programme cover from the 1956 Lancashire Cup final

FINAL FACT

Although Oldham had twice beaten St Helens Recs in Lancashire Cup finals, this was the first ever meeting between Saints and Oldham in a major final.

1958 LANCASHIRE CUP FINAL

SATURDAY 25 OCTOBER at CENTRAL PARK, WIGAN

SAINTS v OLDHAM

SAINTS	OLDHAM
Peter FEARIS *Goal*	Bernard GANLEY (Capt) 2 *Goals*
Tom VAN VOLLENHOVEN	Dick CRACKNELL
Duggie GREENALL	Alan DAVIES *Try*
Ken LARGE	John NOON
Frank CARLTON	John ETTY
Brian HOWARD	Alan KELLETT *DG and Try*
Alex MURPHY	Frank PITCHFORD
Abe TERRY	Ron ROWBOTTOM
Tom McKINNEY	Jack KEITH
Derek BROWN	Ken JACKSON
Walter DELVES	Charlie WINSLADE
Brian BRIGGS	Des McKEOWN
Vince KARALIUS	Derek TURNER
Coach: Jim Sullivan	Coach: Griff Jenkins

Referee: Mr R Gelder (Wakefield) Attendance: 38,780

Saints travelled to the Athletic Grounds in round one and defeated Rochdale Hornets by 20 points to 15. Leigh were beaten 12-2 at Knowsley Road in round two. Saints then defeated Barrow at Craven Park by 18 points to 6 to reach the final.

Oldham were seeking a hat trick of Lancashire Cup final victories having defeated Saints in 1956 and Wigan in 1957. A close contest was expected as the sides occupied the top two positions in the league table going into the match.

The game was a rugged affair with many Saints supporters very unhappy with the Oldham tactics. Tom McKinney had two ribs broken in a foul tackle after just ten minutes and although he bravely carried on he was unable to make any meaningful contribution following his injury. Defences were on top until Kellett unexpectedly dropped a goal after 26 minutes. Peter Fearis evened things up soon afterwards with a penalty but the Saints full back then spilled the ball when attempting to gather in an Oldham kick. Pitchford scooped up the loose ball and passed to Winslade who put Davies in for a try. Ganley's conversion put Oldham 7-2 ahead and there was no further scoring in the first half. Saints had created several try scoring opportunities, but their execution let them down and the chances were spurned.

The longer the second half progressed the less likely it seemed that Saints would score. They only had twelve fit players to Oldham's thirteen and found their opponents' defence unyielding. Ganley kicked another penalty after 55 minutes and Kellett sealed victory when he fly kicked a loose ball and won the race to touch it down. As in the 1956 final Saints had been stifled by Oldham's defence and never played the style of open rugby that had swept many other opponents aside.

SAINTS 2 - OLDHAM 12

The programme cover for the 1958 Lancashire Cup final featured a drawing that would be a familiar sight on many Championship final programmes over the following fifteen years or so.

FINAL FACT

Although Oldham completed a hat trick of Lancashire Cup final victories with this win, they never again won the trophy, losing on all three subsequent final appearances.

1959 LANCASHIRE CUP FINAL

SATURDAY 31 OCTOBER at CENTRAL PARK, WIGAN

SAINTS v WARRINGTON

SAINTS	WARRINGTON
Austin RHODES 2 *Goals*	Eric FRASER (Capt) *Goal*
Tom VAN VOLLENHOVEN	Brian BEVAN *Try*
Duggie GREENALL	Jim CHALLINOR
Brian McGINN	Laurie GILFEDDER
Jan PRINSLOO	Terry O'GRADY
Wilf SMITH	Bobby GREENHOUGH
Alex MURPHY	Jack EDWARDS
Abe TERY	Nat SILCOCK
Tom McKINNEY	Patrick LANNON
Alan PRESCOTT (Capt)	Alistair BRINDLE
Brian BRIGGS	Jack ARKWRIGHT
Dick HUDDART	Harry MAJOR
Fred TERRY	Albert NAUGHTON
Coach: Jim Sullivan	Coach: Cec Mountford

Referee: Mr M Coates (Pudsey)   Attendance: 39,237

Saints were drawn away from home in all three rounds prior to the final. However, they returned victorious from Swinton (17-9), Widnes (24-9) and Whitehaven (18-2) to qualify for the final.

Saints went into the game unbeaten in domestic rugby, their only defeat having been against the Australian touring team.

All the points were scored in an absorbing first half. Austin Rhodes kicked two goals for Saints whilst Fraser managed one for Warrington. However, it was Warrington who scored the game's only try and what a controversial one it was! O'Grady made an excellent sixty yard break and then passed to Greenhough who kicked ahead. Bevan and Tom Van Vollenhoven raced after the ball. Bevan dived and stretched out a hand in an attempt to touch down as Vollenhoven kicked the ball away. Referee Matt Coates adjudged that Bevan had touched the ball before Vollenhoven's boot and to the dismay of Saints' players and supporters awarded the try.

It was not to be Saints' or Vollenhoven's day as the South African was later bundled into touch at the corner flag when attempting to score. This proved to be the closest Saints came to breaking Warrington's hold on the game in a pointless second half.

Bevan was carried off the field shoulder high by jubilant Warrington supporters after the game whilst to this day many Saints supporters claim that the match was decided by a try that should never have been awarded.

SAINTS 4 - WARRINGTON 5

Warrington's Jim Challinor is tackled whilst Alex Murphy looks on. Jim and Alex book went on to coach Saints after retiring from playing.

FINAL FACT

The attendance of 39,237 was never exceeded in any of the subsequent thirty-three Lancashire Cup finals.

1960 LANCASHIRE CUP FINAL

SATURDAY 29 OCTOBER at CENTRAL PARK, WIGAN

SAINTS v SWINTON

SAINTS	SWINTON
Percy LANDSBERG	Ken GOWERS
Tom VAN VOLLENHOVEN *Try*	John SPEED
Ken LARGE *Try*	Peter SMETHURST
Brian McGINN	Alan BUCKLEY
Jan PRINSLOO	Ken McGREGOR *Try*
Austin RHODES *Try and 3 Goals*	George PARKINSON
Alex MURPHY	Tony DYSON
Albert TERRY	Bill BRETHERTON
Bob DAGNALL	Trevor ROBERTS
Fred LEYLAND	Dai MOSES
Don VINES	Ken ROBERTS
Dick HUDDART	Peter NORBURN
Vince KARALIUS (Capt)	Albert BLAN (Capt) *3 Goals*
Coach: Alan Prescott	Coach: Cliff Evans

Referee: Mr E Clay (Leeds) Attendance: 31,755

Saints began their Lancashire Cup campaign with a 19-17 victory at Widnes. Their reward was a home tie against Wigan, which they won by 7 points to 4. They defeated Leigh 15-2 at Hilton Park in the semi-final to earn a place in the final for the third successive year.

Opponents Swinton had not reached the final since World War II, but had assembled a strong team which would compete for major honours during the 1960s. They finished above Saints in third position in the table at the end of the season and topped the Lancashire League.

At this time young men were still called up for conscription into the armed services and consequently Alex Murphy had recently joined the RAF. Saints secured a weekend pass for their star scrum half and he played wonderfully to help Saints to secure victory.

Tom Van Vollenhoven scored the game's opening try in the 11th minute and Ken Large extended the lead with a controversial try. Referee Eric Clay appeared to impede Parkinson as he sought to stop

Large scoring but despite Swinton's protests he awarded the try, which was converted by Austin Rhodes. A Blan penalty completed the first half scoring and Saints led 8-2 at the interval.

Blan kicked two further penalties to bring Swinton to within two points but Rhodes put Saints 10-6 ahead with a penalty kick. He then scored the game's crucial try, which he successfully converted. Swinton did not concede victory however, and winger McGregor scored a try but Blan was unable to land the conversion and the six point deficit proved impossible to bridge so Saints won the trophy for only the second time since the war.

SAINTS 15 - SWINTON 9

FINAL FACT

Three of the Saints backs were South Africans: Percy Landsberg, Tom Van Vollenhoven and Jan Prinsloo.

1961 LANCASHIRE CUP FINAL

SATURDAY 11 NOVEMBER at CENTRAL PARK, WIGAN

SAINTS v SWINTON

SAINTS	SWINTON
Austin RHODES *Try and 5 Goals*	Ken GOWERS
Tom VAN VOLLENHOVEN *Try*	Bernard McMAHON
Ken LARGE *Try*	Bob FLEET
Brian McGINN	Malcolm CUMMINGS
Mick SULLIVAN *Try*	John SPEED
Wilf SMITH	George PARKINSON
Alex MURPHY *Try*	Albert CARTWRIGHT
Albert TERRY	Arnold THOMPSON
Bob DAGNALL	Trevor ROBERTS
Cliff WATSON	Bill BRETHERTON *Try*
Ray FRENCH	Ken ROBERTS
Dick HUDDART	Peter NORBURN
Vince KARALIUS (Capt)	Albert BLAN (Capt) *3 Goals*
Coach: Alan Prescott	Coach: Cliff Evans

Referee: Mr R Gelder (Wilmslow) Attendance: 30,000

Saints were fortunate in receiving home ties in all their matches prior to the final. They had a relatively untroubled passage, defeating Leigh (43-8), Oldham (30-7) and Salford (21-2).

Saints had defeated Swinton 15-9 in the previous year's final and were determined to hold on to the trophy.

The first half was a closely fought affair. Saints went into an early lead with a converted try but Blan pegged them back with two penalty goals. Austin Rhodes then kicked a brace for Saints who consequently led 9-4 at the interval.

Saints cut loose in the second half, scoring four more tries, two of which were converted by Austin Rhodes. Bretherton scored a late consolation try for the Lions, which Blan converted. Saints' backs were far too quick and skilful for the Swinton defence and all of them, apart from Wilf Smith and Brian McGinn, scored tries.

SAINTS 25 - SWINTON 9

LANCASHIRE COUNTY CUP FINAL

ST. HELENS 25

v.

SWINTON 9

SATURDAY, 11th NOVEMBER, 1961

KICK-OFF 2-45 P.M.

The programme cover of 1961 featured a fine view of a packed Central Park taken from the pavilion end of the ground.

FINAL FACT

Eight of the team were locally born: Austin Rhodes, Ken Large, Wilf Smith, Brian McGinn, Alex Murphy, Albert Terry, Bob Dagnall and Ray French

1962 LANCASHIRE CUP FINAL

SATURDAY 27 OCTOBER at CENTRAL PARK, WIGAN

SAINTS v SWINTON

SAINTS	SWINTON
Kel COSLETT 2 *Goals*	Ken GOWERS
Tom VAN VOLLENHOVEN *Try*	Bernard McMAHON
John DONOVAN	Frank HALLIWELL
Wilf SMITH	Alan BUCKLEY
Michael SULLIVAN	John SPEED
Billy BENYON	George PARKINSON
Jeff HEATON	Albert CARTWRIGHT
Jack ARKWRIGHT	Ken ROBERTS
Bob DAGNALL	Trevor ROBERTS
Cliff WATSON	Ron MORGAN
John TEMBEY	Peter NORBURN
Dick HUDDART	Dick BONSER
Bill MAJOR (Capt)	Albert BLAN (Capt) 2 *Goals*
Coach: Stan McCormick	Coach: Cliff Evans

Referee: Mr M Coates (Pudsey) Attendance: 23,523

Two divisions were introduced in the 1962/63 season in an attempt to reinvigorate league games and halt a decline in attendances. Swinton finished six points clear of second placed Saints in the first division to secure the league championship. However, for the third successive year they were defeated by Saints at Central Park in the Lancashire Cup final.

Only three Saints players, Tom Van Vollenhoven, Bob Dagnall and Dick Huddart featured in all three matches. However, no less than seven Swinton players tasted defeat in all three games: Gowers, Speed, Parkinson, Norburn, Blan and Trevor and Ken Roberts.

Saints beat Liverpool City 22-0 in the first round and a 14-3 victory at Blackpool Borough secured an away tie in the semi-final at Oldham. Saints won a close game at Watersheddings by 10 points to 8.

The game was played on a foul day in Wigan. Swinton opted to play into the driving wind and heavy rain in the first half, hoping to profit from the conditions in the second period. The only try of a dour encounter occurred as early as the eighth minute. Prop Ken Roberts looped a pass out just inside his own half. Tom Van Vollenhoven intercepted and raced in for an opportunist try which Kel Coslett converted. The Welsh fullback added a penalty goal in the 24th minute to ensure that Saints led 7-0 at the break.

The pitch became increasingly heavy and the forwards dominated play. Tempers flared five minutes into the second half and props Jack Arkwright and Morgan were dismissed after a bought of fisticuffs. Blan kicked two penalties to reduce the deficit to three points and with the elements in their favour Swinton threw everything at the Saints defensive line but were unable to pierce it and Saints held on to maintain their hold on the trophy.

SAINTS 7 - SWINTON 4

FINAL FACT

The Saints half backs, Billy Benyon and Jeff Heaton, were both only eighteen years of age. Both were local lads who progressed through Saints B and C teams to have long and successful careers at Saints.

1963 LANCASHIRE CUP FINAL

SATURDAY 26 OCTOBER at STATION ROAD, SWINTON

SAINTS v LEIGH

SAINTS	LEIGH
Kel COSLETT 3 *Goals*	Bev RISMAN (Capt)
Len KILLEEN *Try*	Colin TYRER 2 *Goals*
Tom VAN VOLLENHOVEN *Try*	Gordon LEWIS
Keith NORTHEY	Mike COLLINS
Peter HARVEY	Tony LEADBETTER
Wilf SMITH *Try*	Austin RHODES
Alex MURPHY	Terry ENTWISTLE
John TEMBEY	Bill ROBINSON
Bob DAGNALL	John LEWIS
Cliff WATSON	Stan OWEN
Ray FRENCH	Mick MURPHY
Keith ASHCROFT	Mick MARTYN
Bill MAJOR (Capt)	Derek HURT
Coach: Alan Prescott	Coach: Jack Helme

Referee: Mr R Gelder (Warrington) Attendance: 21,231

The first round draw ensured that there would not be a fourth successive Saints v Swinton final as the two sides were paired to play each other at Station Road. Saints prevailed by 12 points to 2 and then easily beat Workington Town 28-4 at Knowsley Road. They overcame Warrington 21-14 at Wilderspool in the semi-final to reach the final for the sixth successive year.

Opponents Leigh had been relegated from the first division the previous season and entered the game as huge underdogs, despite having beaten Wigan in the second round. Long standing Saints favourite Austin Rhodes featured in the Leigh ranks, whilst prop Stan Owen would transfer to Saints later in the season.

Leigh started strongly and Tyrer landed two penalty goals to put them in front 4-0. A Kel Coslett penalty then put Saints on the scoreboard. Just before half time Len Killeen scored the game's first try and although Coslett could not land the conversion Saints went to the dressing room with a one point advantage.

Kel Coslett put Saints further ahead with a penalty goal and then Tom Van Vollenhoven, playing in the centre, scored a good try. Coslett's conversion made the score 12-4 to Saints and when Wilf Smith finished off a flowing move to score Saints' third try the contest was as good as over. Leigh tried hard until the final whistle, with Risman causing the Saints defence a few problems but Saints held out without too much trouble to record their fourth successive Lancashire Cup final victory.

SAINTS 15 - LEIGH 4

Somewhat surprisingly, the programme cover featured an action photograph from a Great Britain v Australia match

FINAL FACT

Saints' three-quarter line was comprised entirely of rugby union converts. Len Killeen and Tom Van Vollenhoven had both played union in South Africa whilst Keith Northey and Peter Harvey had both played for local union clubs before signing for Saints.

1964 LANCASHIRE CUP FINAL

SATURDAY 24 OCTOBER at CENTRAL PARK, WIGAN

SAINTS v SWINTON

SAINTS	SWINTON
Frank BARROW	Ken GOWERS 2 *Goals*
Tom PIMBLETT	David HARRIES
Keith NORTHEY	Bob FLEET
Billy BENYON *Try*	Alan BUCKLEY
Len KILLEEN 3 *Goals*	John SPEED
Peter HARVEY	George PARKINSON
Alex MURPHY (Capt)	Graham WILLIAMS
John TEMBEY	Harold BATE
Bob DAGNALL	Derek CLARKE
John WARLOW	Ken HALLIWELL
Ray FRENCH	Graham REES
Mervyn HICKS *Try*	Barry SIMPSON
Duggie LAUGHTON	Derek HURT
Substitutes	Substitutes
Tony BARROW	Bill DAVIES
Cliff WATSON	Albert CARTWRIGHT
Coach: Stan McCormick	Coach: Cliff Evans

Referee: Mr E Clay (Leeds) Attendance: 17,383

The 1964/65 season saw Saints reach their seventh successive Lancashire Cup final and achieve their fifth consecutive final victory.

Saints reached the final despite receiving away draws in each of the three previous rounds. They visited Knotty Ash in the first round and defeated perennial strugglers Liverpool City 41-11 before travelling to Craven Park to meet Barrow in round two. A 22-11 victory meant that they had to play Warrington at Wilderspool in the semi-final. A hard fought 10-8 win put them through to the final.

Swinton had reached their fourth final in five years but unfortunately for them their opponents were always Saints and they were once again unable to taste victory. Gowers, Speed and Parkinson played in all four matches and must have been thoroughly sick of collecting losers' medals. In contrast, Bob Dagnall was only the Saints player to play in all four finals against Swinton.

A Gowers penalty put Swinton into the lead but Len Killeen squared things up by also kicking a penalty. As half time approached the match was evenly poised until Billy Benyon latched onto a Ray French pass to dive over for a try, which Killeen converted.

The second half continued to be a tight, forward dominated affair. Bob Dagnall hooked the ball from thirteen of the twenty keenly contested scrums and this helped Saints to control the game and to wear their opponents down with basic no frills rugby. Killeen's third goal extended Saints' lead and thirteen minutes from the end Saints finally made their pressure pay when Mervyn Hicks crashed over. A Gowers penalty completed the scoring.

SAINTS 12 - SWINTON 4

The cover of the 1964 final programme featured an action shot from one of the earlier Saints v Swinton finals.

FINAL FACT

Saints' five successive victories were based on resolute defence and incisive attack. Over the five games they only conceded two tries, and both came late in games that were already won. In contrast Saints scored fourteen tries, all but the final one by Hicks scored by backs.

1967 LANCASHIRE CUP FINAL

SATURDAY 7 OCTOBER at CENTRAL PARK, WIGAN

SAINTS v WARRINGTON

SAINTS	WARRINGTON
Frank BARROW	Keith AFFLECK
Tom VAN VOLLENHOVEN (Capt)	John COUPE
Alan WHITTLE	John MELLING
Billy BENYON	Peter HARVEY
Tony BARROW	Brian GLOVER
Peter DOUGLAS	Willie ASPINALL (Capt) *Goal*
Tommy BISHOP	Parry GORDON
John WARLOW	Keith ASHCROFT
Bill SAYER	Dave HARRISON
Cliff WATSON	Brian BRADY
Brian HOGAN	Ken PARR
John MANTLE	Barry BRIGGS
Kel COSLETT *Goal*	Ray CLARKE
Substitutes	Substitutes
Peter GARTLAND	Joe PICKAVANCE
Tony KARALIUS	Joe PRICE
Coach: Joe Coan	Coach: Jackie Fleming

Referee: Mr G F Lindop (Wakefield) Attendance: 16,897

Central Park had been the scene of four Saints Lancashire Cup victories over Swinton in the 1960s. Saints supporters gathered at the familiar surroundings on a grey, damp October day hoping for a similarly successful outcome against Warrington.

Saints had squeezed past Rochdale Hornets by 7 points to 4 at Knowsley Road in the first round and were fortunate enough to secure a bye in round two. They travelled to Swinton in the semi-final and won a tight game by 12 points to 8.

Almost 17,000 supporters gathered to watch the final. The programme stated that 'Both teams are playing attractive football this season and we can expect a fast and exciting match.' Unfortunately, the exceptionally heavy pitch meant that the spectacle was not fast but the closeness of the game provided some excitement.

Try scoring chances were few and far between. Saints captain Tom Van Vollenhoven was tackled into touch by the corner flag just before he could get the ball down, whilst Warrington winger Brian Glover turned inside with a clear run to line in front of him and the chance was lost.

Only two minutes of the first half remained when Warrington stand-off Aspinall landed a goal to give the Wire a slender advantage at half time.

Saints evened things up when Kel Coslett kicked a penalty seven minutes into the second period. The match was punctuated by well over forty scrums and became a complete stalemate as the clinging mud made forward progress almost impossible. Coslett had two chances to kick penalty goals late in the game but lifting the heavy ball out of the mud was difficult and neither kick was successful. In truth, neither side really deserved a victory.

SAINTS 2 - WARRINGTON 2

LANCASHIRE COUNTY CUP FINAL

ST. HELENS 2 v WARRINGTON 2

*

Photograph from last meeting of todays Finalists at Central Park, 1959

CENTRAL PARK
WIGAN

SATURDAY 7th OCTOBER 1967

KICK-OFF 3-0 pm

OFFICIAL PROGRAMME - SHILLING

The programme cover featured a photograph from the 1959 final showing Brian Bevan being tackled into touch near the corner flag. The touch judge is wearing a blazer, which was still common practice at the time.

FINAL FACT

This was only the second drawn Lancashire Cup final in history. The other took place in the very first final in 1905 when Wigan and Leigh played out a 0-0 draw.

1967 LANCASHIRE CUP FINAL REPLAY

SATURDAY 2 DECEMBER at STATION ROAD, SWINTON

SAINTS v WARRINGTON

SAINTS	WARRINGTON
Frank BARROW	Tom CONROY
Tom VAN VOLLENHOVEN (Capt)	John COUPE
Wilf SMITH	John MELLING *Try*
Billy BENYON	Bill ALLEN 2 *Goals*
Les JONES *Try*	Brian GLOVER
Peter DOUGLAS	Tony SCAHILL
Tommy BISHOP	Parry GORDON *Try*
John WARLOW *Try*	Keith ASHCROFT
Bill SAYER	Dave HARRISON
Cliff WATSON	Joe PRICE
Eric CHISNALL *Try*	Ken PARR
John MANTLE	Barry BRIGGS
Kel COSLETT	Ray CLARKE
Substitutes	Substitutes
John HOUGHTON 2 Goals	Peter HARVEY
Joe EGAN	Bill CHURM
Coach: Joe Coan	Coach: Jackie Fleming

Referee: Mr G F Lindop (Wakefield) Attendance: 7,577

The sides had drawn 2-2 in the original game on 7 October. It was eight weeks before the match could be replayed, mainly due to fixture congestion exacerbated by the Australian tour of Great Britain. Only 7,577 turned up at Station Road in Swinton to watch, less than half the attendance at the original game. Eight years earlier over 39,000 had watched the two sides meet in the 1959 final!

The weather was reasonably kind and the replay was much more open than the original final. Les Jones opened the scoring in the 28th minute when he touched down in the corner after good work by Wilf Smith and Billy Benyon. Warrington levelled things up with a Melling try just before half time.

Two minutes after the break Gordon just evaded a desperate cover tackle by Tom Van Vollenhoven to score Warrington's second try and a good conversion by Allen put Warrington 8-3 ahead. Seven minutes later Saints drew level when John Warlow barged over near the posts and John Houghton converted. Eric Chisnall then showed quick thinking to play the ball to himself, a legal move at the time, and plunge over for a try. However, Allen reduced the deficit to a single point by kicking a penalty goal with eight minutes left. The match remained in the balance right until Houghton kicked a penalty for Saints just before the end to secure a 13-10 victory.

SAINTS 13 -WARRINGTON 10

LANCASHIRE COUNTY RUGBY LEAGUE

* **ST. HELENS** 13

versus

WARRINGTON 10

On Swinton R.F.C. Ground, Station Road, Swinton
nr. Manchester

SATURDAY, 2nd, DECEMBER, 1967

KICK-OFF 3 p.m.

OFFICIAL PROGRAMME - ONE SHILLING

The programme cover from the 1967 final replay

FINAL FACT

This was Saints legend Tom Van Vollenhoven's last season.
It was the only occasion that he captained a winning side in a final.

1968 LANCASHIRE CUP FINAL

FRIDAY 25 OCTOBER at CENTRAL PARK, WIGAN

SAINTS v OLDHAM

SAINTS	**OLDHAM**
Austin RHODES	Martin MURPHY
Frank WILSON 2 *Tries*	Mike ELLIOTT
Billy BENYON	Phil LARDER
Frank MYLER	Jim McCORMACK
Cen WILLIAMS *Try*	Derek WHITEHEAD *Goal*
Alan WHITTLE	Wilf BRIGGS
Tommy BISHOP (Capt) *Try*	Tom CANNING
John WARLOW	Ken WILSON
Bill SAYER	Kevin TAYLOR
Cliff WATSON	Geoff FLETCHER (Capt)
Graham REES *Try*	Bob IRVING
Eric CHISNALL *Try*	Charlie McCOURT
Kel COSLETT 6 *Goals*	Arthur HUGHES
Substitutes	Substitutes
John HOUGHTON	Trevor BUCKLEY
Brian HOGAN	Dennis MADERS
Coach: Cliff Evans	Coach: Gerry Helme

Referee: Mr W Thompson (Huddersfield) Attendance: 17,008

Saints were drawn at home against Wigan in the first round and won a close game by 19 points to 16. This was followed by a trip to Naughton Park where Widnes were beaten 20-17. Saints travelled to Hilton Park in the semi-final and defeated Leigh 17-6 to reach the final.

Oldham had defeated Saints in the 1956 and 1958 finals and had hopes of making it a trio of wins in 1968. They were captained by Geoff Fletcher, who for many years had a pig farm next to Saints' Knowsley Road ground.

The final was played under the Central Park floodlights on a Friday evening and the first forty minutes were very closely fought. The only score in the first half was a penalty from Whitehead.

The second half was an entirely different story. Kel Coslett levelled things up with a penalty goal and then Saints cut loose, scoring six second half tries without reply as they completely overran their opponents. Coslett converted all but one of the tries and having struggled to breach the Oldham defence in the first half, Saints rattled up thirty unanswered second half points to run out very comfortable winners.

Coach Cliff Evans was delighted to be on the winning side, having coached Swinton to four Lancashire Cup final defeats against Saints earlier in the decade.

SAINTS 30 - OLDHAM 2

FINAL FACT

The sixties was an exceptionally fruitful decade for Saints in the Lancashire Cup. They reached the final seven times and won the lot, although a replay was required in 1967.

1970 LANCASHIRE CUP FINAL

SATURDAY 28 NOVEMBER at STATION ROAD, SWINTON

SAINTS v LEIGH

SAINTS	LEIGH
Frank BARROW	Stuart FERGUSON 2 *Goals*
Les JONES	Rod TICKLE
Billy BENYON	Les CHISNALL
John WALSH	Mick COLLINS
Frank WILSON	Joe WALSH
Frank MYLER	David ECKERSLEY *Try*
Alan WHITTLE	Alex MURPHY (Capt)
Albert HALSALL	Dave CHISNALL
Tony KARALIUS	Kevin ASHCROFT
Graham REES	Derek WATTS
John MANTLE	Paul GRIMES
Eric CHISNALL	Geoff CLARKSON
Kel COSLETT 2 *Goals*	Mick MOONEY
Substitutes	Substitutes
Jeff HEATON	Tom CANNING
Eric PRESCOTT	Roy LESTER
Coach: Jim Challinor	Player Coach: Alex Murphy

Referee: Mr W Thompson (Huddersfield) Attendance: 10,775

Saints' Lancashire Cup campaign started win an easy 30-3 victory at Alt Park against Huyton. Swinton visited Knowsley Road in round two and were defeated by 20 points to 7. A crowd of 23,508 packed into Central Park for the semi-final against Wigan and Saints recorded a superb 23-0 victory and as a result went into the final as favourites. However, Alex Murphy had put together a strong team at Leigh and most supporters expected a close, hard fought contest and that is what they got.

The match was not a great advertisement for the game. Defences were on top throughout and Billy Thompson had a hard time controlling two very aggressive teams as tempers flared. Not a single point was scored in the first half.

Three Chisnall brothers started the match but only Eric remained on the field at the final whistle as Leigh players Les and Dave were both sent off, along with Saints' scrum half Alan Whittle. Eckersley scored the game's only try, whilst Kel Coslett and Ferguson each slotted over two goals.

Alex Murphy was both the player-coach and the captain of Leigh and was delighted to defeat his old club in the final. Later in the season Leigh would shock Leeds at Wembley and bring home the Challenge Cup.

SAINTS 4 - LEIGH 7

LANCASHIRE COUNTY RUGBY LEAGUE

versus

ST. HELENS 4

On Swinton R.F.C. Ground, Station Road, Swinton
nr. Manchester

SATURDAY, 28th NOVEMBER, 1970

KICK-OFF 3-15 p.m.

OFFICIAL PROGRAMME - ONE SHILLING

The red rose featured on the majority of Lancashire Cup final programmes when the venue was Swinton

FINAL FACT

Saints went to Hilton Park just two days after the final and knocked Leigh out of the BBC2 floodlit trophy, winning by 10 points to 4.

1982 LANCASHIRE CUP FINAL

SATURDAY 23 OCTOBER at CENTRAL PARK, WIGAN

SAINTS v WARRINGTON

SPONSOR: FORSHAWS BURTONWOOD BREWERY

SAINTS	WARRINGTON
Brian PARKES	Steve HESFORD 2 *Goals*
Barrie LEDGER	Paul FELLOWS *Try*
Chris ARKWRIGHT	Ron DUANE
Roy HAGGERTY	John BEVAN
Denis LITHERLAND	Mike KELLY *Try*
Steve PETERS	Paul CULLEN
Neil HOLDING	Ken KELLY (Capt) *Try*
Mel JAMES	Neil COURTNEY
Graham LIPTROT	Carl WEBB
Gary BOTTELL	Tony COOKE
Gary MOORBY	Bob ECCLES *Try*
Peter GORLEY	John FIELDHOUSE
Harry PINNER (Capt)	Mike GREGORY
Substitutes	Substitutes
John SMITH	Derek FINNEGAN
Roy MATHIAS	Dave CHISNALL
Coach: Billy Benyon	Coach: Kevin Ashcroft

Referee: Mr J Holdsworth (Leeds) Attendance: 6,462

Saints had triumphed in some very close matches to claim a place in the final for the first time since 1970. A late Peter Gorley try enabled them to defeat Widnes at Naughton Park 14-12 and they squeezed past Barrow 9-6 in the second round. They could only draw 7-7 with Carlisle at Knowsley Road in the semi-final but managed to win the replay in Cumbria 9-5.

Coach Billy Benyon had selected a seriously under strength side to play Australia the previous weekend and this had contributed significantly to a 0-32 defeat. The gamble failed to play off as his full strength side similarly failed to register a point against a determined Warrington side.

The county cup finals failed to really capture supporters' interest in the 1970s and early 1980s and the attendance was the lowest of Saints' Lancashire Cup final appearances.

The first half was an attritional one, with few try scoring opportunities. The only score was a Fellows try. Hesford hoisted a high kick and chased and caught it before sending out a pass which Fellows took at full stretch to score in the corner.

Saints failed to turn a period of early second half pressure into points. Warrington then extended their lead when Hesford caught the ball when it rebounded off a Saints player and put winger Kelly over in the corner. Hesford missed both conversions but kicked a penalty to put the Wire 8-0 ahead. Saints' victory prospects were diminished further when Graham Liptrot was dismissed for a bad foul on Webb. Eccles extended Warrington's lead with their third try and then Ken Kelly scored the best try of the game under the posts. Hesford converted to seal a comfortable victory for Warrington.

SAINTS 0 - WARRINGTON 16

Man of the match: Steve Hesford

The 1982 Lancashire Cup competition was sponsored by Forshaws, the owners of Burtonwood brewery. Warrington received £3,000 from the sponsors for winning the final.

FINAL FACT

Steve Hesford was adjudged to be the man of the match despite missing seven out of nine kicks at goal and not scoring a try.

1984 LANCASHIRE CUP FINAL

SUNDAY 28 OCTOBER at CENTRAL PARK, WIGAN

SAINTS v WIGAN

SPONSOR: FORSHAWS BURTONWOOD BREWERY

SAINTS	WIGAN
Phil VEIVERS	Shaun EDWARDS
Barrie LEDGER	John FERGUSON
Shaun ALLEN	David STEPHENSON
Mal MENINGA *2 Tries*	Colin WHITFIELD *3 Goals*
Sean Day *Try and 5 Goals*	Henderson GILL *Try*
Chris ARKWRIGHT	Mark CANNON
Neil HOLDING	Jimmy FAIRHURST
Tony BURKE	Neil COURTNEY
Graham LIPTROT	Nicky KISS *Try*
Peter GORLEY	Brian CASE
Andy PLATT	Graeme WEST (Capt) *Try*
Paul ROUND	Shaun WAYNE
Harry PINNER (Capt)	Ian POTTER
Substitutes	Substitutes
John SMITH	John PENDLEBURY
Roy HAGGERTY *Try*	Mick SCOTT
Coach: Billy Benyon	Coaches: Colin Clarke/Alan McInnes

Referee: Mr R Campbell (Widnes) Attendance: 26,074

1984/85 will always be known as Mal Meninga's season. The Australian superstar made a tremendous impact on the club and he easily won the man of the match award in the final.

Saints negotiated the first two rounds safely before the arrival of Meninga and his team mate Phil Veivers from Australia, hammering Runcorn Highfield 58-14 at Knowsley Road and defeating holders

Barrow 26-10 at Craven Park. Both Australians contributed tries in a 31-10 home victory over Leigh in the semi-final.

Although this was Wigan's 30th appearance in the final and Saints' 16th they had only met each other once before in the final, back in 1953.

For the first time ever the final was played on a Sunday. Interest in game was very high. The attendance was largest for a Lancashire Cup final since 1961 and was more than the combined attendances of the previous three finals.

Only seven minutes had passed when Mal Meninga scored the opening try of the game, first selling a splendid dummy and then demonstrating immense power to bulldoze over in the corner. Sean Day landed a superb conversion. Two minutes later Whitfield kicked a penalty for Wigan, but Saints continued to put pressure on the home side's defence and Paul Round looked certain to score but Ferguson's cover tackle hauled him down short of the line. However, from the play the ball Meninga sent Roy Haggerty in for try which Day converted to put Saints 12-2 ahead. In the 35th minute Meninga put Sean Day over for a try which the winger converted and when Meninga scored his second try just before the break, which Day once again converted, the match seemed as good as over.

However, Wigan did not want be embarrassed by their bitter rivals on home turf and played much better in the second half. Gill's try, converted by Whitfield, made the score 24-8 and then captain West narrowed the gap to twelve points with another try. Kiss scored Wigan's third try and Whitfield's conversion set Saints' supporters nerves jangling but Day landed a penalty and Saints ran out 26-18 winners.

Saints players and supporters were delighted that the club's seven year long wait for a trophy was over at last.

SAINTS 26 - WIGAN 18

Man of the match: Mal Meninga

FINAL FACT

This was the first time ever that the Lancashire Cup Final had not been played at a neutral venue. Warrington's Wilderspool ground had originally been selected to host the final but Saints and Wigan both considered that its 16,000 capacity would be insufficient. Wigan won the toss to decide which club would have home advantage and the controversial decision was vindicated when over 26,000 spectators turned up at Central Park.

1991 LANCASHIRE CUP FINAL

SUNDAY 20 OCTOBER at WILDERSPOOL, WARRINGTON

SAINTS V ROCHDALE HORNETS   SPONSOR: GREENALL'S

SAINTS	ROCHDALE HORNETS
David TANNER	Colin WHITFIELD (Capt) *Goal*
Mike RILEY	Phil FOX
Gary CONNOLLY	Darren ABRAM *Try*
Tea ROPATI	Ronnie DUANE *Try*
Anthony SULLIVAN	Tony GARRITY
Phil VEIVERS 2 *Tries*	Brett CLARK
Paul BISHOP *Try and 2 Goals*	Steve GARTLAND
Jonathan NEILL	Tony HUMPHRIES
Paul GROVES	Martin HALL
Kevin WARD	Bob MARSDEN
John HARRISON	Cliff ECCLES
George MANN 2 *Tries*	Paul OKESENE
Shane COOPER (Capt)	Mike KUITI *Try*
Substitutes	Substitutes
Mark BAILEY	Matt CALLAND
Paul FORBER	Simon BAMBER
Coach: Mike McClennan	Coach: Stan Gittins

Referee: David Campbell (Widnes)   Attendance: 9,269

Saints reached their first Lancashire Cup final for seven years in 1991. However, the wait had been much longer for opponents Rochdale Hornets. Their previous appearance had been in 1965 and they had not won the trophy since the 1918/19 season.

Saints scored over a century of points in the first round, defeating Trafford Borough by the astonishing score of 104-12, which included twelve goals from stand in goal kicker Bernard Dwyer. Saints were given a sterner test by Oldham in round two, but won a free flowing game 39-26. Saints and Wigan fans hoped that the semi-final draw would keep them apart but it was not to be. Saints were given home advantage and won a spectacular game 28-16 in front of a crowd of over 17,000 at Knowsley Road. By contrast just 1,900 watched Hornets defeat Carlisle 19-6 in the other semi-final.

Many Saints supporters headed off to Warrington thinking that victory was a foregone conclusion but a spirited Rochdale side clearly had other ideas. They took the lead in the 13th minute when Duane touched down after good work from Whitfield and Kuiti. Saints replied with a Phil Veivers try but Hornets established a 10-4 lead when Abram scored their second try. Paul Bishop scored Saints second try but again could not land the conversion and underdogs Rochdale led 10-8 at half time.

Five minutes after the break Bishop sent Veivers in for his second try and kicked the conversion. Saints were ahead for the first time in the game. George Mann struck a killer blow when he capitalised on Gartland's fumble to score and Bishop's conversion put Saints 20-10 ahead. Rochdale refused to lie down and Kuiti's try reduced the deficit to six points. However, Saints steadied the ship and Phil Veivers put Mann in for his second try to seal a 24-14 victory.

SAINTS 24 - ROCHDALE HORNETS 14

Man of the match: Bob Marsden

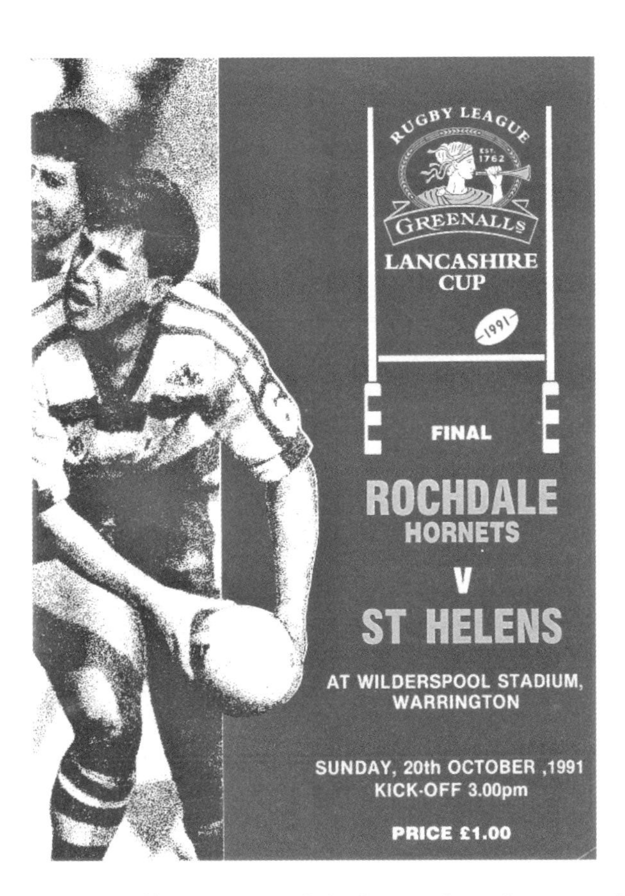

Another brewery, Greenall's, sponsored the Lancashire Cup in its final few years. Their total prize money in 1991 was £24,500, with the winners pocketing £6,250.

FINAL FACT

Referee David Campbell dismissed Saints scrum half Paul Bishop after the final whistle for allegedly stamping on former Saints half back Brett Clarke.

1992 LANCASHIRE CUP FINAL

SUNDAY 18 OCTOBER at KNOWSLEY ROAD, ST HELENS

SAINTS v WIGAN

SPONSOR: GREENALL'S

SAINTS	WIGAN
Phil VEIVERS	Steve HAMPSON
Alan HUNTE	Jason ROBINSON
Gary CONNOLLY	Joe LYDON
Jarrod McCRACKEN	Andrew FARRAR
Anthony SULLIVAN	Martin OFFIAH
Tea ROPATI	Frano BOTICA 2 *Goals and DG*
Jonathan GRIFFITHS	Shaun EDWARDS
John HARRISON	Kelvin SKERRETT
Bernard DWYER 2 *Goals*	Martin DERMOTT
Kevin WARD	Andy PLATT
Chris JOYNT	Denis BETTS
Sonny NICKLE	Billy McGINTY
Shane COOPER (Capt)	Dean BELL (Capt)
Substitutes	Substitutes
Gus O'DONNELL	Martin CROMPTON
Paul FORBER	Neil COWIE
Coach: Mike McClennan	Coach: John Monie

Referee: Stuart Cummings (Widnes)

Attendance: 20,534

Such was the interest in the final between old rivals Saints and Wigan that no neutral Rugby League venue in Lancashire was large enough to hold the expected crowd. Therefore, as in 1984, the two clubs tossed a coin to decide which would have home advantage. This time Saints won the toss, but as in 1984 the visiting side won the trophy.

Saints coasted past third division strugglers Barrow in the first round, winning 36-2. Widnes presented an altogether stiffer challenge in the second round and it took a late Tea Ropati try to claim a 10-8 victory. Salford led Saints in the semi-final at Knowsley Road before falling away to lose 5-18.

Wigan's progress to the final was carefree. The draw paired them with three second division sides and they racked up 162 points, conceding just 16.

The final took place just six days before the World Cup final between Great Britain and Australia, with eleven of the participating players in the British squad. Nonetheless the two sides played out a no holds barred, bone jarring struggle in front of the capacity crowd.

Defences were on top throughout and every metre gained had to be fully earned. With try scoring chances at a premium, Botica opted to kick a drop goal as early as the 12th minute. He added two successful penalty kicks to put the visitors 5-0 ahead. The encounter was tough and uncompromising from start to finish and referee Cummings sent Kevin Ward and Edwards to the sin bin after a scuffle shortly before half time.

Try as they might neither side could pierce the other's defence and it was Saints' turn to convert penalties into points, Bernard Dwyer landing two after indiscretions from Lydon and Cowie, to reduce the deficit to a single point. A minute from time tempers boiled over again and Sonny Nickle and Bell were sent to the sin bin. Wigan held on to win an unremittingly tense encounter by 5 points to 4.

SAINTS 4 - WIGAN 5

Man of the match: Denis Betts

FINAL FACT

This proved to be the last ever Lancashire Cup final. It was decided to reduce the number of fixtures played, especially by the leading clubs; Saints played 40 games in the 1992/93 season and Wigan played 46. Consequently the county cup competitions were scrapped after being an integral part of the Rugby League season for 87 years.

WESTERN REGION CHAMPIONSHIP FINAL

- This competition only existed for two seasons, 1962/63 and 1963/64. This coincided with the short lived two division experiment and was designed to give second division clubs the opportunity to play some local first division clubs and so have the potential to improve their attendance receipts. The competition was in effect the Lancashire League Championship and the participants were the twelve Lancashire clubs plus Whitehaven and Workington Town from Cumberland. Each club played four other teams home and away. A league table was compiled from these results and a top four play-off was then undertaken, with the winning semi-finalists competing in the final.

- Saints beat Swinton in the 1963/64 final by 10 points to 7 at Central Park, Wigan. The attendance was 17,363.

Saints 1963/64 squad

Back row (left to right): Tom Van Vollenhoven, Ray French, Mervyn Hicks, Bob Dagnall, John Warlow, Cen Williams, Kel Coslett,

Front row (l to r): Len Killeen, Wilf Smith, Alex Murphy, John Tembey, Keith Ashcroft, Brian Todd,

The team won the Lancashire Cup and the Western Region Championship.

1964 WESTERN REGION CHAMPIONSHIP FINAL

SATURDAY 16 MAY at CENTRAL PARK, WIGAN

SAINTS v SWINTON

SAINTS	**SWINTON**
Kel COSLETT 2 *Goals*	Ken GOWERS
Tom VAN VOLLENHOVEN	John SPEED *Try*
Cen WILLIAMS	Bob FLEET
Keith NORTHEY *Try*	George PARKINSON
Len KILLEEN	John STOPFORD
Peter HARVEY	Graham WILLIAMS
Alex MURPHY	Albert CARTWRIGHT
John TEMBEY (Capt)	Harold BATE
Bob BURDELL	Derek CLARKE
Stan OWEN	Ken HALLIWELL
Ray FRENCH *Try*	Ron MORGAN
John WARLOW	Graham REES
Duggie LAUGHTON	Albert BLAN (Capt) 2 *Goals*
Coach: Stan McCormick	Coach: Cliff Evans

Referee: Mr E Clay (Leeds) Attendance: 17,363

The concept of Eastern and Western Divisional Championships only lasted for two seasons. The 1964/65 season saw a return to a single league table with the league championship play-offs expanded to include the top sixteen teams. This format remained until two divisions were re-introduced in 1973/74, albeit without the accompanying regional championships.

The Western Division comprised the twelve Lancashire clubs together with the two from Cumberland. Fixtures were arranged so as to provide second division sides with fixtures against sides from the first division. Saints played Barrow, Liverpool City, Salford and Whitehaven home and away, winning all eight matches whilst scoring a total of 173 points and only conceding 57. They finished in second place in the Western Division table and defeated third placed Oldham 22-11 at Knowsley Road in the semi-final. Swinton, who were the season's first division champions for the second successive year, also finished top of the Western Division table and beat fourth placed Widnes in the other semi-final.

Both sides had a key player missing. Saints hooker Bob Dagnall was suspended whilst Swinton's star centre Alan Buckley had been injured playing in a local workshop competition during the week before the final. However, Saints welcomed back Tom Van Vollenhoven after a month's absence due to injury.

Saints made a dream start when in only the second minute Duggie Laughton made a superb break and passed to Keith Northey who raced in for a try, which Kel Coslett converted. The rest of the first half was a rather dour affair. Swinton dominated scrum possession but made few inroads into a determined Saints defence. The only other points came when Coslett kicked a penalty goal in the 24th minute.

Veteran Blan kicked a penalty soon after the restart to get the Lions onto the scoreboard. The game continued in much the same vein as in the first half until a dramatic last ten minutes. Swinton finally got their speedy backs more involved and Stopford finished off the best move of the day by scoring an excellent try, which Blan converted to bring the sides level.

As the clock wound down a replay was looking increasingly likely until Alex Murphy darted through a gap. However, he slipped and lost his footing but managed to get away a pass to John Warlow who then fed John Tembey. With the defence desperately trying to cover the move he found Ray French in support. The second rower slipped out of a tackle and galloped twenty-five yards to touch down. Although Coslett missed the conversion there was very little time remaining and soon afterwards Eric Clay blew his whistle for full time.

SAINTS 10 - SWINTON 7

FINAL FACT

The divisional championships were amongst the strangest competitions devised in the history of the game. The match programme stated that 'The winners will be included in the Official Guide under the list of County League Championship Winners. The West Region competition is in effect the Lancashire League Championship.'

BBC2 FLOODLIT TROPHY FINALS

This competition was launched in 1965 and ran for fifteen seasons until 1979 when it was abolished as part of the BBC's financial cutbacks. Only eight teams participated in the first season but more and more installed floodlights and the number had risen to 22 by 1979. The majority of matches were televised on Tuesday evenings in the autumn and early winter, with the final usually taking place in December. Although the format changed slightly over the years as the number of clubs competing increased, it was basically an unseeded knock-out competition.

- Saints played in seven finals, winning two and losing five.
- Saints' highest score was 22 v Dewsbury (1976)
- Opponents' highest score was 26 v Hull KR (1977)
- Saints' biggest margin of victory was 20 v Dewsbury (1976)
- Saints' biggest margin of defeat was 15 v Hull KR (1977)
- The highest attendance at any BBC2 Floodlit Trophy Final in which Saints have played is 13,479 v Wigan (1968)
- The lowest attendance at any BBC2 Floodlit Trophy Final in which Saints have played is 3,858 v Dewsbury (1976).
- Only two of the fifteen finals had neutral venues, and Saints participated in neither of them. Of the seven finals in which Saints appeared, four were held at Knowsley Road. The other three venues were Central Park, Wigan (1968), Headingley, Leeds (1970) and Craven Park, Hull (1977)

The BBC2 Floodlit Trophy

Programme

Published by the ST. HELENS RUGBY F.C. LTD.

DIRECTORS

H. B. COOK, (Chairman) F. C. DROMGOOLE (Vice-Chairman)
F. S. BROWN, S. HALL, H. J. HUNTER, C. MARTIN, A. NAYLOR,
J. ROBINSON, H. STOTT, L. SWIFT, F. YEARSLEY, J. YEARSLEY
J. SEDDON, Company Sec. B. LOWE, Club Sec.

B.B.C. 2 FLOOD-LIT COMPETITION FINAL

ST. HELENS 0

versus

* CASTLEFORD 4

Tuesday, 14th December, 1965

Kick-off 7-25 p.m.

Price - - - Threepence

The programme cover for the very first BBC2 Floodlit Competition final. There was nothing very special about the programme, as it was simply the standard Saints programme of the period which could read from cover to cover in less than five minutes. The Saints player is wearing the standard kit of the period. At this time the 'red vee' was reserved for Wembley appearances.

1965 BBC2 FLOODLIT TROPHY FINAL

TUESDAY 14 DECEMBER at KNOWSLEY ROAD, ST HELENS

SAINTS v CASTLEFORD

SAINTS	CASTLEFORD
Frank BARROW	Derek EDWARDS
Tom VAN VOLLENHOVEN	Colin BATTYE
David WOOD	Malcolm BATTYE
Bill BENYON	Ron WILLETT 2 *Goals*
Len KILLEEN	Trevor BRIGGS
Alex MURPHY (Capt)	Alan HARDISTY (Capt)
Bob PROSSER	Roger MILLWARD
Ray FRENCH	Abe TERRY
Bob DAGNALL	Johnnie WARD
Cliff WATSON	Clive DICKINSON
Mervyn HICKS	Bill BRYANT
John MANTLE	John TAYLOR
Doug LAUGHTON	Peter SMALL
Substitutes	Substitutes
Peter HARVEY	Trevor BEDFORD
Frank WARD	John WALKER
Coach: Joe Coan	Coach: George Clinton

Referee: Mr L Gant (Wakefield) Attendance: 11,510

The BBC2 Floodlit Trophy competition was played for the first time on eleven consecutive Tuesday evenings between 5 October and 14 December 1965. The second half of each match was televised live on the new BBC2 channel. As only seven clubs possessed floodlights, Leeds were invited to make up the number of participants to eight.

Each team played two matches in the preliminary play-offs and the four with the best points differences met in the semi-finals. Saints opened the tournament with a thrilling 25-19 victory over Leigh and subsequently defeated Leeds 21-9 to finish with what proved to be the second best points difference.

Their reward was a home semi-final against Swinton which Saints won 9-5. As Saints had finished above Castleford in the qualifying competition they were able to host the final.

Saints were expected to win as they had already defeated Castleford twice in the league and in fact were undefeated in all league matches played so far that season. However, the Yorkshire side defended exceptionally well throughout the match and blunted Saints' attacking edge. The only score of the first half was a Willett penalty in the 26th minute. Len Killeen had a rare off night and was unable to kick either of his penalty attempts.

Willett kicked another penalty in the 49th minute and try as they might Saints could make little headway against a resolute Castleford defence. Tom Van Vollenhoven managed one clean break but full back Edwards covered across and tackled him into touch. Killeen had two further attempts at goal but neither was successful and with time running out Saints resorted to 'up and unders' in a fruitless attempt to score but Castleford held on to record a deserved victory and secure the £1,000 prize money and the shiny new trophy.

SAINTS 0 - CASTLEFORD 4

FINAL FACT

Castleford went on to win the first three Floodlit Trophy competitions, beating Swinton in the 1966 final and Leigh in 1967.

1968 BBC2 FLOODLIT TROPHY FINAL

TUESDAY 17 DECEMBER at CENTRAL PARK, WIGAN

SAINTS v WIGAN

SAINTS	**WIGAN**
Cen WILLIAMS	Colin TYRER 2 *Goals*
Frank WILSON	Bill FRANCIS
Bill BENYON	Eric ASHTON (Capt)
Frank MYLER	Bill ASHURST
John WILLS	Peter ROWE
Alan WHITTLE	Cliff HILL *Try*
Tommy BISHOP (Capt)	Johnny JACKSON
John WARLOW	John STEPHENS
Bill SAYER	Colin CLARKE
Cliff WATSON	Keith MILLS
John MANTLE	Terry FOGERTY
Brian HOGAN	Kevin O'LOUGHLIN
Kel COSLETT 2 *Goals*	Doug LAUGHTON
Substitutes	Substitutes
Eric PRESCOTT	Geoff LYON
Eric CHISNALL	Steve PRICE
Coach: Cliff Evans	Coach: Eric Ashton

Referee: Mr Eric Clay (Leeds) Attendance: 13,479

The Floodlit Trophy was in its fourth season in 1968. The number of clubs taking part had risen to eighteen and so a preliminary round was played with two ties in order to reduce the number of teams to sixteen for the first round. Saints drew Barrow in the preliminary round which was played over two legs. Saints won 21-5 at Knowsley Road before losing 11-18 at Craven Park but won the tie 32-23 on aggregate. All Saints' other ties were at home. They defeated Swinton 12-10, Hull 14-10 and Warrington 29-6 to reach the final. Only diehard supporters went to watch the games live, with less than 22,000 in total attending the five games.

Wigan were in good form and topped the league table, having only lost one of their first nineteen matches and were hopeful of beating Saints for the very first time in a cup final, especially as they were given home advantage.

As was almost always the case in December, the playing surface was muddy and both sides found it difficult to play with their usual attacking flair. Kel Coslett managed to kick two penalty goals in challenging conditions whilst Tyrer kicked one for the home side. Just before half time an almighty fight broke out between Brian Hogan and Bill Ashurst and referee Clay had little option but to send both players off.

Although both teams came out for the second half in clean shirts within minutes they were once again caked in mud as the war of attrition continued. Despite there being only twenty four players on the field chances were few and it looked like Saints would hold on for victory but with just three minutes left Cliff Watson knocked on when trying to pass out of a tackle. Wigan stand-off Hill scooped up the loose ball and raced away to score near the posts. Tyrer converted and Wigan held on to win the trophy for the only time in its fifteen year history.

SAINTS 4 - WIGAN 7

FINAL FACT

Incredibly, Brian Hogan, who was sent off for fighting, transferred to Wigan just four days after the final. Within a month he played for Wigan against Saints and was once again sent off!

1970 BBC2 FLOODLIT TROPHY FINAL

TUESDAY 15 DECEMBER at HEADINGLEY, LEEDS

SAINTS v LEEDS

SAINTS	LEEDS
Frank BARROW	John HOLMES 2 *Goals*
Les JONES *Try*	Alan SMITH
Billy BENYON	Sid HYNES (Capt) *Try and Goal*
John WALSH	Ronnie COWAN
Frank WILSON	John ATKINSON
Alan WHITTLE	Tony WAINWRIGHT
Jeff HEATON	Mick SHOEBOTTOM
Graham REES	John BURKE
Tony KARALIUS	Tony FISHER
Eric CHISNALL	Ted BARNARD
John MANTLE	Bob HAIGH
Eric PRESCOTT	Bill RAMSEY
Kel COSLETT (Capt) *Goal*	Ray BATTEN
Substitutes	Substitutes
Frank MYLER	John LANGLEY
Bill SHEFFIELD	Bob ECCLES
Coach: Jim Challinor	Coach: Derek Turner

Referee: Mr E Lawrinson (Warrington) Attendance: 7,612

Saints had beaten Castleford 14-7 at Knowsley Road in the first round and their reward was a trip to Hilton Park where they defeated Leigh by ten points to four. The semi-final was an epic affair against Wigan. The first match at Central Park resulted in a 7-7 draw and so the sides had to replay at Knowsley Road, where Saints managed to win a very tight game by 16 points to 15.

Saints went into the final as underdogs for two reasons. Firstly, it was their fifth game in eleven days, as the need to replay the semi-final had added to an already very busy schedule. Secondly, the fact that Leeds had undersoil heating, which more or less guaranteed that the match could be played no matter how cold the evening was, meant that the Yorkshire side received home advantage.

Nonetheless, Saints started strongly and took the lead after ten minutes when Eric Chisnall broke through and found Billy Benyon in support. The centre fed Les Jones who cut inside the Leeds cover defence to score a fine try. However, Kel Coslett missed the conversion and Hynes reduced the lead to a single point when he landed a penalty. The Leeds captain then scored a try which Holmes converted to put the home side 7-3 up at the break.

Although Saints dominated possession from the scrums, winning twenty-four of the forty which packed down, their attack failed to fire on the chilly evening. Holmes extended Leeds' lead with another penalty and although Coslett, who had missed three goal attempts in the first half, finally managed to put one between the posts, Leeds held on to win the trophy in what proved to be their only final appearance in the fifteen years of the competition's existence.

SAINTS 5 - LEEDS 9

FINAL FACT

Due to power shortages the electricity authorities refused to allow the Headingley floodlights to be switched on. The only illumination available was from the BBC's own lights, which were designed only to boost the floodlighting. Much of the playing area was very poorly lit and despite Jim Challinor's protests the match continued to its gloomy conclusion.

1971 BBC2 FLOODLIT TROPHY FINAL

TUESDAY 14 DECEMBER at KNOWSLEY ROAD, ST HELENS

SAINTS v ROCHDALE HORNETS

SAINTS	**ROCHDALE HORNETS**
Geoff PIMBLETT	Joe CHAMBERLAIN *Goal*
Les JONES	Norman BRELSFORD
Bill BENYON	Jim CRELLIN
John WALSH	David TAYLOR
Frank WILSON	Brian GLOVER
Ken KELLY	Frank MYLER (Capt)
Jeff HEATON	Peter GARTLAND
Graham REES	Peter BIRCHALL
Tony KARALIUS	Peter CLARKE
Eric CHISNALL	Eddie BROWN
Eric PRESCOTT	Bob WELDING
John MANTLE	Bill SHEFFIELD
Kel COSLETT Capt) *4 Goals*	Henry DELOOZE
Substitutes	Substitutes
John HOUGHTON	John HAMMOND
John STEPHENS	Alan HODKINSON
Coach: Jim Challinor	Player Coach: Frank Myler

Referee: Mr E Clay (Leeds)   Attendance: 9,300

Saints began their BBC Trophy campaign at Station Road, where they defeated Swinton 14-9. They beat Leigh at Hilton Park by 13 points to 4 in round two. Saints produced a marvellous performance in the semi-final at Headingley and registered an excellent 17-0 victory. After three tough away games they were delighted to receive home advantage in the final.

Saints had appeared in three of the previous six finals but had been narrowly defeated in all of them. However, Saints supporters were confident that their team had the ability to break their duck against little fancied Rochdale Hornets. The visitors had four ex-Saints players in their ranks, Frank Myler, Brian Glover, Bill Sheffield and Peter Gartland.

Points were always at a premium in BBC trophy finals, with a total of only 68 being scored in the previous six finals. The 1971 final was a similarly tight affair, with no tries being scored. The sides had the two best defensive records in the league at the end of the season, each conceding an average of less than nine points a game over the thirty-four games of the league campaign.

The game was an attritional affair, with defences on top throughout. The four tackle rule in operation at the time contributed to the inability of either side to put prolonged pressure on their opponents' line. Chamberlain put Hornets ahead with a penalty goal but Kel Coslett landed two for Saints to earn them a narrow 4-2 first half advantage.

The game continued in a similar vein after the break but two further successful kicks from captain Coslett edged Saints into an 8-2 lead and despite plenty of honest endeavour from Rochdale they were unable to break down a well organised Saints defence and the trophy finally rested in Saints' hands after the disappointments of 1965, 1968 and 1970.

SAINTS 8 - ROCHDALE HORNETS 2

FINAL FACT

Remarkably, there were only two changes made from the starting 13 that took to the field in the previous year's BBC2 final defeat against Leeds. Geoff Pimblett replaced Frank Barrow at full back and Ken Kelly played stand-off in place of Alan Whittle.

1975 BBC2 FLOODLIT TROPHY FINAL

TUESDAY 16 DECEMBER at KNOWSLEY ROAD, ST HELENS

SAINTS v DEWSBURY

SAINTS	DEWSBURY
Geoff PIMBLETT 2 *Goals*	John LANGLEY
Les JONES	John HEGARTY
Billy BENYON *Try*	Graham CHALKLEY
David HULL *Try*	Ian SIMPSON
Roy MATHIAS 2 *Tries*	Garry MITCHELL
Frank WILSON *Try*	Nigel STEPHENSON *Goal*
Jeff HEATON *DG*	Alan BATES
John MANTLE	Harry BEVERLEY
Tony KARALIUS	Ray PRICE
Mel JAMES	Steve HANKINS
George NICHOLLS	Steve HALLORAN
Eric CHISNALL	Graham BELL
Kel COSLETT (Capt) *Goal*	Jeff GRAYSHON
Substitutes	Substitutes
David ECKERSLEY	Steve LEE
Graham LIPTROT	Phil ARTIS
Coach: Eric Ashton	Coach: Dave Cox

Referee: Mr W Thompson (Huddersfield) Attendance: 3,858

22 clubs entered the 1975 BBC floodlit competition, compared to just eight ten years earlier. Saints had to play in the preliminary round and won by 15 points to 7 at Rochdale Hornets. They were fortunate to be drawn at home in the remainder of the competition. They defeated Whitehaven 38-10 and Hull 36-13 before edging a closely fought semi-final against Barrow by 11 points to 9.

Injuries forced Saints to play Welsh three-quarter Frank Wilson at stand-off but he relished the challenge and was one of their most influential players.

This was a game that Saints dominated from start to finish, scoring five tries to nil and only stubborn defence from Dewsbury prevented a landslide victory. Kel Coslett opened the scoring with a fifth minute penalty and Jeff Heaton edged Saints further ahead with a drop goal. Despite putting the Yorkshire side under near constant pressure the game was half an hour old when their defence was finally breeched. Billy Benyon's long pass put David Hull over. The dry conditions suited Saints very well and soon afterwards Roy Mathias scored Saints' second try, which Coslett converted to put Saints 11-0 ahead at the interval.

After a quarter of an hour of the second half Hull sent Benyon over to extend Saints' lead. Stephenson ensured that Dewsbury did not remain scoreless when he opted to kick a penalty but a splendid Saints try in the 68th minute ensured that they would be comfortable winners. Geoff Pimblett split the tiring Dewsbury defence and passed to Mathias, who raced in for his second try. Frank Wilson deservedly scored the final try of the game and Pimblett kicked the conversion. Saints' twenty point margin of victory was the widest ever in a Floodlit Trophy final.

Coach Eric Ashton declared that 'I only hope that this success gives us the confidence to go and win something else in the New Year.' His hopes were realised as Saints went on to lift the Challenge Cup and the Premiership Trophy in 1976.

SAINTS 22 - DEWSBURY 2

FINAL FACT

The paltry attendance of 3,858 was the lowest at any major final in Rugby League history.

A housing development has been built on the site of the old Knowsley Road ground.
This monument has been erected to ensure that the historical importance of the site is not forgotten.

(© Copyright Ken Bold)

Tony Karalius was inducted into the Saints Past Players Hall of Fame in 2004. George Nicholls presents him with a framed photograph.

1977 BBC2 FLOODLIT TROPHY FINAL

TUESDAY 13 DECEMBER at CRAVEN PARK, HULL

SAINTS v HULL KINGSTON ROVERS

SAINTS	HULL KINGSTON ROVERS
Geoff PIMBLETT (Capt)	Dave HALL 4 *Goals*
Les JONES	Ged DUNN 2 *Tries*
Derek NOONAN	Mike SMITH *Try*
Eddie CUNNINGHAM *Try*	Bernard WATSON
Peter GLYNN 2 *Tries and Goal*	Clive SULLIVAN *Try*
Bill FRANCIS	Steve HARTLEY *Try*
Ken GWILLIAM	Roger MILLWARD (Capt)
Dave CHISNALL	John MILLINGTON
Graham LIPTROT	David WATKINSON
Mel JAMES	John CUNNINGHAM
Mick HOPE	Phil LOWE
Tony KARALIUS	Paul ROSE *Try*
Harry PINNER	Len CASEY
Substitutes	Substitutes
Billy PLATT	Alan AGAR
Neil COURTNEY	Mike HUGHES
Coach: Eric Ashton	Player Coach: Roger Millward

Referee: Mr M Naughton (Widnes) Attendance: 10,099

Saints hammered Dewsbury 51-0 at Knowsley Road in the first round. Leigh provided much stiffer opposition in round two, but Saints prevailed 14-7 at Hilton Park. Saints hosted Salford in the semi-final and won a tight contest by 7 points to 4.

A trip to Craven Park presented a difficult challenge as Hull KR had put together arguably the strongest side in their history. They had a fearsome pack and their skilful backs included all-time greats Roger Millward and Clive Sullivan. Saints badly missed international forwards Eric Chisnall and George Nicholls.

Hull KR started strongly and Smith scored an early try. However, Peter Glynn, who had moved to full back following an injury to Geoff Pimblett, squared things up with a good try. Veteran Sullivan gave Rovers the lead when he touched down in the 17th minute. The home side were now dominating proceedings and Rose played the ball to himself and scored another try. Hall's first successful conversion put KR 11-3 ahead at the break.

The Rovers pack continued to have the upper hand in the second half and prop Millington barged over to extend their lead. Hull KR were now completely in control and their speedy backs proved to be more and more dangerous. Winger Dunn scooted in for a rapid brace of tries and Hall's three second half conversions put KR 26-3 ahead. Saints managed to avoid a complete rout. Glynn, arguably their best player on the night, scored his second try and landed the conversion. Eddie Cunningham added a late try but Saints were a well beaten side. Hull KR won the trophy for what was to be the only occasion. The £5,000 winners' cheque was a welcome bonus.

SAINTS 11 - HULL KINGSTON ROVERS 26

Hull KR are nicknamed 'The Robins', presumably because their shirts have a red band across the chest. A cartoonist managed to turn a little robin into a rather terrifying rugby figure on the cover of the match programme.

FINAL FACT

The BBC2 Trophy final rarely attracted a bumper crowd. However, the attendance exceeded 10,000 for the first time since 1969.

1978 BBC2 FLOODLIT TROPHY FINAL

TUESDAY 12 DECEMBER at KNOWSLEY ROAD, ST HELENS

SAINTS v WIDNES

SAINTS	WIDNES
Geoff PIMBLETT 2 *Goals*	David ECKERSLEY
Les JONES	Stuart WRIGHT 2 *Tries*
Peter GLYNN	Eric HUGHES
Eddie CUNNINGHAM	Mal ASPEY
Roy MATHIAS	P SHAW
Bill FRANCIS	Mick BURKE *Try and 2 Goals*
Neil HOLDING	Reg BOWDEN
Dave CHISNALL *Try*	Brian HOGAN
Graham LIPTROT	Keith ELWELL
Mel JAMES	Jim MILLS
George NICHOLLS	Mick ADAMS
John KNIGHTON	Alan DEARDEN
Harry PINNER	Doug LAUGHTON
Substitutes	Substitutes
Eric CHISNALL	John MYLER
Chris ARKWRIGHT	Glynn SHAW
Coach: Eric Ashton	Player Coach: Doug Laughton

Referee: Mr J McDonald (Wigan) Attendance: 10,250

Saints had to play a preliminary round tie at Knowsley Road, defeating Warrington 13-9. Saints won 17-15 at The Willows, Salford in round one and Castleford were swept aside 47-5 at Knowsley Road in round two. Saints' reward was a difficult trip to the Boulevard in the semi-final but a resolute performance enabled them to beat Hull 13-5.

Despite Saints having home advantage in the final, Widnes entered the game as slight favourites, having knocked Saints out of the John Player trophy earlier in the month, one of four defeats in Saints' previous five games. Although it was not yet Christmas, this was already Saints' 24th game of the season.

Saints started well and after a spell of pressure Bill Francis scythed through the Widnes defence and found Eric Chisnall in support. He sold a dummy and went in for an excellent try which Geoff Pimblett converted. However, Widnes fought back and Hughes' pass found Wright in acres of space and the speedy wingman touched down. Burke pulled his conversion attempt wide. The Widnes stand-off made amends when he collected a long pass to score a fine try and his conversion went over after striking a post to give Widnes an 8-5 lead at half time.

With twenty minutes left Pimblett reduced the gap to a single point when he landed a penalty but Burke restored his side's three-point advantage with another successful kick. As the final whistle approached a Widnes grubber kick eluded Roy Mathias and Wright was on hand to touch down and seal victory for the visitors.

SAINTS 7 - WIDNES 13

The Line-up

ST. HELENS

Colours: White jersey with Red 'V' White Shorts

1. GEOFF PIMBLETT, *Full Back*
2. L. JONES/~~B. PARKES~~, *Right Wing*
3. PETER GLYNN, *Right Centre*
4. E. CUNNINGHAM/~~C. ARKWRIGHT~~,
5. ROY MATHIAS, *Left Wing*
6. BILL FRANCIS, *Stand Off*
7. NEIL HOLDING, *Scrum Half*
8. DAVE CHISNALL, *Front Row*
9. G. LIPTROT/~~M. SMITH~~, *Hooker*
10. MEL JAMES, *Front Row*
11. GEORGE NICHOLLS, *Second Row*
12. JOHN KNIGHTON, *Second Row*
13. HARRY PINNER, *Loose Forward*

Substitutes:
14.
15. CHISNALL E

T	G	D/G	Pts

WIDNES

Colours: White Jersey Black Shorts

1. DAVID ECKERSLEY, *Full Back*
2. STUART WRIGHT, *Right Wing*
3. ERIC HUGHES, *Right Centre*
4. MAL ASPEY, *Left Centre*
5. GLYNN SHAW, *Left Wing*
6. MICK BURKE, *Stand Off*
7. REG BOWDEN, *Scrum Half*
8. BRIAN HOGAN, *Front Row*
9. KEITH ELWELL, *Hooker*
10. JIM MILLS, *Front Row*
11. MICK ADAMS, *Second Row*
12. A. DEARDEN/G. SHAW, *Second Row*
13. DOUG LAUGHTON, *Loose Forward*

Substitutes:
14. JOHN MYLER
15.

T	G	D/G	Pts

Referee: Mr. J. McDonald (Wigan)
Touch Judges: Mr. B. Baker and Mr. T. Dawes

Programme edited by G. Sutcliffe
Filmset and printed Litho by Lockie Press Ltd., Golborne, Nr. Warrington. Lancs.

WELCOME TO KNOWSLEY RD.

SAINTS REVIEW

The Official Match Day Magazine of St. Helens Rugby League Football Club Ltd.

THE RUGBY FOOTBALL LEAGUE

BBC 2 Floodlit Trophy Final

SAINTS v. WIDNES
Tuesday, 12th December, 1978
Kick-off 7.30 p.m.

Programme 15p

The back and front covers of the 1978 BBC2 Floodlit Trophy final programme. My father liked to record team changes, scorers and the scoring sequence on programmes. On this occasion he didn't record the names of two of the substitutes, probably because they didn't get onto the field during the game.

FINAL FACT

This was the fourth and last time that Knowsley Road hosted the BBC2 Floodlit Trophy final. Saints won two of these, in 1971 and 1975, but lost in both 1965 and 1978. They lost all three finals which were played at their opponents' grounds.

STATISTICS AND TRIVIA

ALL FINALS

Saints have played in 79 finals, two of which have required replays.

They have won 42 and lost 37.

- The finals have been in nine different competitions: Challenge Cup (21), Super League Grand Final (10), Championship (9), Premiership (9), Club Championship (1), Regal Trophy (2), Lancashire Cup (19), Western Region Championship (1) and BBC2 Floodlit Trophy (7)

- Saints' highest score in a final is 44 (1959 Championship Final v Hunslet). Opponents' highest score is 48 (1992 Premiership Final v Wigan).

- Saints' biggest margin of victory is 30 (2006 Challenge Cup v Huddersfield Giants) Opponents' biggest margin is 34 (1915 Challenge Cup Final v Huddersfield)

- Saints have failed to score at all in three finals: v Castleford (1965 BBC2 Floodlit Trophy Final), v Warrington (1982 Lancashire Cup Final) and v Wigan (1989 Challenge Cup Final)

- Saints have never 'nilled' an opponent in a final. However, they have restricted them to just two points on eight occasions.

- Saints' biggest margin of defeat is 34 (1915 Challenge Cup v Huddersfield)

VENUES

The 81 matches (79 finals and two replays) have been played at a total of seventeen venues. In the list below venues in italics no longer exist.

- Bradford (Odsal Stadium) P2 W2 (2 Championship Finals 1959 W, 1970 W)
- Cardiff (Millennium Stadium) P1 W1 (Challenge Cup Final 2004 W)
- Edinburgh (Murrayfield) P1 L1 (Challenge Cup Final 2002 L)
- Huddersfield (McAlpine Stadium) P1 L1 (Regal Final 1996 L)
- *Hull (Craven Park)* P1 L1 (BBC Final 1978 L)
- Leeds (Elland Road) P1 W1 (Premiership Final 1985 W)

- Leeds (Headingley) P3 D1 L2 (Challenge Cup Final 1897 L; Championship Final 1967 D; BBC Final 1970 L)
- London (Twickenham) P2 W2 (Challenge Cup Finals 2001 W, 2006 W)
- London (Wembley Stadium) P15 W9 L6 (Challenge Cup Finals 1930 L, 1953 L, 1956 W, 1961 W, 1966 W, 1972 W, 1976 W, 1978 L, 1987 L, 1989 L, 1991 L, 1996 W, 1997 W, 2007 W, 2008 W)
- *Manchester (Maine Road)* P1 W1 (Championship Final 1953 W)
- Manchester (Old Trafford) P15 W6 L9 (Premiership Finals 1988 L, 1992 L, 1993 W, 1996 L, 1997 L; Super League Grand Finals 1999 W, 2000 W, 2002 W, 2006 W, 2007 L, 2008 L, 2009 L, 2010 L, 2011 L, 2014 W)
- *Oldham (Watersheddings)* P1 L1 (Challenge Cup Final 1915 L)
- *St Helens (Knowsley Road)* P5 W2 L3 (BBC Finals 1965 L, 1971 W, 1976 W, 1978 L; Lancashire Cup Final 1992 L)
- *Swinton (Station Road)* P13 W7 L6 (Lancashire Cup Finals 1952 L, 1953 W, 1958 L, 1963 W, 1967 Replay W, 1970 L; Championship Finals 1965 L, 1966 W, 1967 Replay L, 1971 W, 1972 L; Premiership Finals 1976 W, 1977 W)
- Wakefield (Belle Vue) P1 W1 (Championship Final 1932 W)
- *Warrington (Wilderspool)* P2 W2 (Lancashire Cup Finals 1926 W, 1991 W)
- *Wigan (Central Park)* P16 W8 D1 L7 (Lancashire Cup Finals 1932 L, 1956 L, 1959 L, 1960 W, 1961 W, 1962 W, 1964 W, 1967 D, 1968 W, 1982 L, 1984 W; Western Region Final 1964 W; BBC Final 1968 L; Club Championship Final 1974 L; Premiership Final 1975 L; John Player Final 1988 W)

OPPONENTS

Saints have played 21 different opponents in finals:

- Batley P1 L1 (Challenge Cup Final 1897 L)
- Bradford Bulls P5 W5 (Challenge Cup Finals 1996 W, 1997 W, 2001 W; Super League Grand Finals 1999 W, 2002 W)
- Castleford P1 L1 (BBC Final 1965 L)
- Catalans Dragons P1 W1 (Challenge Cup Final 2007 W)
- Dewsbury P1 W1 (BBC Final 1976 W)
- Halifax P5 W3 L2 (Championship Finals 1953 W, 1965 L, 1966 W; Challenge Cup Finals 1956 W, 1987 L)
- Huddersfield P4 W2 L2 (Challenge Cup Finals 1915 L, 1953 L, 2006 W*; Championship Final 1932 W) *Played as Huddersfield Giants
- Hull FC P2 W2 (Super League Grand Final 2006 W; Challenge Cup Final 2008 W)
- Hull Kingston Rovers P2 W1 L1 (BBC Final 1977 L; Premiership Final 1985 W)
- Hunslet P1 W1 (Championship Final 1959 W)

- Leeds P11 W3 L8 (Championship Finals 1970 W, 1972 L; BBC Final 1970 L; Challenge Cup Finals 1972 W, 1978 L; Premiership Final 1975 L; John Player Final 1988 W; Super League Grand Finals 2007 L*, 2008 L*, 2009 L*, 2011 L*) *Played as Leeds Rhinos
- Leigh P3 W1 L2 (Lancashire Cup Finals 1952 L, 1963 W, 1970 L)
- Oldham P3 W1 L2 (Lancashire Cup Finals 1956 L, 1958 L, 1968 W)
- Rochdale Hornets P2 W2 (BBC Final 1971 W; Lancashire Cup Final 1991 W)
- Salford P1 W1 (Premiership Final 1976 W)
- St Helens Recreation P1 W1 (Lancashire Cup Final 1926 W)
- Swinton P5 W5 (Lancashire Cup Finals 1960 W, 1961 W, 1962 W, 1964 W; Western Region Final 1964 W)
- Wakefield Trinity P1 L1 (Championship Final 1967 L, in a replay)
- Warrington P6 W2 L4 (Lancashire Cup Finals 1932 L, 1959 L, 1967 W, in a replay, 1982 L; Club Championship Final 1974 L; Premiership Final 1977 W)
- Widnes P4 W1 L3 (Challenge Cup Finals 1930 L, 1976 W; BBC Final 1978 L; Premiership Final 1988 L)
- Wigan P19 W9 L10 (Lancashire Cup finals 1953 W, 1984 W, 1992 L; Challenge Cup Finals 1961 W, 1966 W, 1989 L, 1991 L, 2002 L*, 2004 W*; Championship final 1971 W; Premiership Finals 1992 L, 1993 W, 1996 L, 1997* L; BBC Final 1968 L; Regal Trophy Final 1996 L; Super League Grand Finals 2000 W*, 2010 L*, 2014 W*) *Played as Wigan Warriors

AVERAGE ATTENDANCES

Below are the average attendances at Saints' finals in the various competitions. The number in brackets refers to the total number of finals involving Saints that were played (including replays).

- Challenge Cup Finals (21) 72,897
- Super League Grand Finals (10) 65,673
- Championship Finals (10) 30,040
- Premiership Finals (9) 25,838
- Lancashire Cup Finals (20) 24,078
- Club Championship Final (1) 18,556
- Western Region Final (1) 17,363
- John Player/Regal Finals (2) 17,130
- BBC2 Floodlit Finals (7) 9,444

MAN OF THE MATCH AWARDS

Man of the Match awards were largely unheard of until after the Second World War, when the Lance Todd Trophy was presented to the Man of the Match after the Challenge Cup Final. From 1965 The Harry Sunderland Trophy was presented to the Man of the Match after the Championship Final. It has subsequently been presented after the Club Championship Final, the Premiership Final and the Super League Grand Final. The John Player/Regal trophy had a Man of the Match award throughout its 25 year history. A Man of the Match award was introduced in 1974 for the Lancashire Cup Final and continued to be awarded in all subsequent finals. There was no official award in any of The BBC2 Floodlit Trophy finals or in the two Western Region Finals played.

Lance Todd Trophy, Challenge Cup Final

1953 Peter Ramsden (Huddersfield)

1956 Alan Prescott

1961 Dick Huddart

1966 Len Killeen

1972 Kel Coslett

1976 Geoff Pimblett

1978 George Nicholls

1987 Graham Eadie (Halifax)

1989 Ellery Hanley (Wigan)

1991 Denis Betts (Wigan)

1996 Robbie Paul (Bradford Bulls)

1997 Tommy Martyn

2001 Sean Long

2002 Kris Radlinski (Wigan Warriors)

2004 Sean Long

2006 Sean Long

2007 Leon Pryce and Paul Wellens

2008 Paul Wellens

Harry Sunderland Trophy, Championship Final

1965 Terry Fogarty (Halifax)

1966 Albert Halsall

1967 Ray Owen (Wakefield Trinity)

1970 Frank Myler

1971 Bill Ashurst (Wigan)

1972 Terry Clawson (Leeds)

Club Championship Final

1974 Barry Philbin (Warrington)

Premiership Final

1975 Mel Mason (Leeds)

1976 George Nicholls

1977 Geoff Pimblett

1985 Harry Pinner

1988 David Hulme (Widnes)

1992 Andy Platt (Wigan)

1993 Chris Joynt

1996 Andrew Farrell (Wigan)

1997 Andrew Farrell (Wigan)

Super League Grand Final

1999 Henry Paul (Bradford Bulls)

2000 Chris Joynt

2002 Paul Deacon (Bradford Bulls)

2006 Paul Wellens

2007 Rob Burrow (Leeds Rhinos)

2008 Lee Smith (Leeds Rhinos)

2009 Kevin Sinfield (Leeds Rhinos)

2010 Thomas Leuluai (Wigan Warriors)

2011 Rob Burrow (Leeds Rhinos)

2014 James Roby

John Player/Regal Trophy Final

1988 Paul Loughlin

1996 Keiron Cunningham

Lancashire Cup Final

1982 Steve Hesford (Warrington)

1984 Mal Meninga

1992 Denis Betts (Wigan)

- Man of the Match awards have been awarded in 49 finals in which Saints have participated.
- Saints players have won these awards on 24 occasions. Players from the opposing team have won them on 25 occasions.
- Saints players have won the Lance Todd trophy on twelve occasions, opposition players have won it six times.
- Sean Long has won the trophy on three occasions (2001, 2004, 2006).
- Paul Wellens has won it twice, although he had to share it with Leon Pryce in 2007.
- Chris Joynt is the only Saints player to have won the Harry Sunderland Trophy twice.
- Saints players have only won the Harry Sunderland Trophy in nine of the 26 finals in which Saints have competed.
- George Nicholls, Geoff Pimblett and Paul Wellens have won both the Lance Todd and Harry Sunderland trophies.

OTHER MAJOR TROPHIES WON

Just for the record the following major trophies have been won by Saints in competitions that did not include a final.

Super League

For its first two seasons the Super League champions were the team which finished at the top of the table. Saints won the inaugural Super League title in 1996, pipping Wigan by a single point.

First Division Championship

Between 1962/63 and 1963/64 and also between 1973/74 and 1994/95 the team finishing top of the table were declared the First Division Champions. Saints were First Division Champions on only one occasion, in 1974/75.

League Leaders' Shield

This was first awarded in 1964/65. Prior to this there was no official recognition given to the side that finished at the top of the league table. It was not awarded between 1973/74 and 1997, as the teams that finished top during this period were awarded the Championship trophy. Saints have won the Shield on seven occasions: 1964/65, 1965/66, 2005, 2006, 2007, 2008, 2014 and 2018.

Lancashire League

The Lancashire League was an annual competition from 1895 to 1970 for professional teams from Lancashire. Teams from Cheshire and Cumbria also competed in the league on occasions. During the period 1896-1901 the county leagues were played as there was no national league championship. From 1901 until 1970 they were played alongside the Championship. Saints won the Lancashire League on eight occasions: 1929/30, 1931/32, 1952/53, 1959/60, 1964/65, 1965/66, 1966/67 and 1968/69.

World Club Challenge

Saints have won this trophy twice. On both occasions their opponents were Brisbane Broncos and both games were played at the Reebok Stadium, the home of Bolton Wanderers FC. In 2001 Saints won by 20 points to 18 and in 2007 they won 18-14.

European Championship

This competition only lasted for one season, 1970/71. Saints, champions of England, played against St Gaudens, the champions of France. Saints won 30-11 in France and then crushed their opponents 62-0 at Knowsley Road to complete a 92-11 aggregate victory. The wide margin of victory and the poor attendances at the games meant that the competition was abandoned.

MY OWN TOP TEN FINALS

I'm sure every Saints supporter could come up with their own list of favourites, so to get the ball rolling here is mine. Most were in my lifetime but I've chosen others because of their historical significance.

1. 1996 Challenge Cup Final: Saints 40 Bradford Bulls 32
2. 2002 Super League Grand Final: Saints 19 Bradford Bulls 18
3. 1956 Challenge Cup Final: Saints 13 Halifax 2
4. 1959 Championship Final: Saints 44 Hunslet 22
5. 1971 Championship Final: Saints 16 Wigan 12
6. 1897: Challenge Cup Final: Saints 3 Batley 10
7. 2004: Challenge Cup Final: Saints 32 Wigan Warriors 16
8. 1926: Lancashire Cup Final: Saints 10 St Helens Recs 2
9. 2006: Super League Grand Final: Saints 26 Hull 4
10. 1961: Challenge Cup Final: Saints 12 Wigan 6

ACKNOWLEDGEMENTS

This is my first book and I have needed the advice and support of a number of individuals and organisations in order to write and publish it.

Alex Service, the Saints historian, has provided some very useful guidance. Patsy Byron from Stellar Books has steered me through the process of turning a manuscript into a published book. Sig Kasatkin from rlphotos, Andrew Varley, Alex Service and the Saints Heritage Society have all provided images. I have been unable to discover who, if anyone, is the copyright holder for some images in the book. If copyright holders exist and declare themselves I will be very happy to acknowledge them in any future edition.

I have used many reference materials in compiling this book. The most important of these have been: *Rothmans Rugby League Yearbook 1982/83 to 1999* by Raymond Fletcher and David Howes, *Rugby League Yearbook 2003/04 to 2016/17* edited by Tim Butcher and *St Helens Rugby League Club* by Alex Service and David Whittle

Whilst I have tried very hard to avoid making any mistakes or inaccuracies it is almost inevitable that the book may contain some. If this is the case please accept my apologies.